EARLY KOREAN LITERATURE

EARLY KOREAN LITERATURE

SELECTIONS AND INTRODUCTIONS

David R. McCann

COLUMBIA UNIVERSITY PRESS ▲ NEW YORK

The author wishes to thank *Korean Studies* (Center for Korean Studies, University of Hawaii) for permission to use revised versions of "The Story of Ch'ŏyong, a Parable of Literary Negotiation" (vol. 21, 1997) and "Chinese Diction in Korean *Shijo* Verse" (vol. 17, 1993).

Materials from *Form and Freedom in Korean Poetry* (Leiden: E. J. Brill, 1988) used with permission of the publisher.

Quotation on page 149 from *The Woman Warrior* by Maxine Hong Kingston
Copyright © 1975, 1976 by Maxine Hong Kingston
Reprinted by permission of Alfred A. Knopf, a Division of Random House, Inc.

Columbia University Press wishes to express its appreciation for assistance given by the Pushkin Fund toward the cost of publishing this book.

Columbia University Press
Publishers Since 1893
New York Chichester, West Sussex
Copyright © 2000 Columbia University Press

Library of Congress Cataloging-in-Publication Data
Early Korean literature : selections and introductions / David R. McCann.
    p. cm.
   Includes bibliographical references and index.
    ISBN 0-231-11946-1 (cloth)—ISBN 0-231-11947-X (paper)
    1. Korean literature—Translations into English—To 1900. 2. Korean
  literature—History and criticism—To 1900.   I. McCann, David R. (David
  Richard), 1944–
PL984.E1 E27 2000
895.7'08001—dc21   99-053800

♾

Casebound editions of Columbia University Press books are printed on permanent and durable acid-free paper.
Designed by Chang Jae Lee
Printed in the United States of America
c 10 9 8 7 6 5 4 3 2 1
p 10 9 8 7 6 5 4 3 2 1

IN MEMORY

To my friend, colleague, mentor, and fellow translator,
Marshall Pihl, I dedicate this book.

THE SILLA MONK WŎLMYŎNG COMPOSED THE
FOLLOWING *HYANGGA* SONG, THE *"CHE MANGMAE KA,"*
OR "SONG IN MEMORY OF MY YOUNGER SISTER."

Here on the path of life-to-death
I stay, afraid, while you have gone
without even saying you might go.
Leaves blown in autumn winds
this way and that; we who once
grew on one branch do not know,
any of us, where we are going.
I shall prepare the way
to the Land of Amitabha, and there,
There I shall wait.

CONTENTS

The experience of designing and teaching a course at Cornell University, "Introduction to Korea," encouraged my interest in exploring history through literature, and vice versa, while focusing my attention on such matters as the ways in which written works, whether poems or dynastic histories, are summaries of previous and complex cultural, political, or aesthetic negotiations. Reading a poem, a story, a legend or myth, a part of a historical record, or a newspaper editorial from the late nineteenth century, the students and I would begin by asking, "If this was the answer, what was the question?" What, for example, might Wang Kŏn, founder of the Koryŏ dynasty, have had on his mind when he stated shortly before he died, in the second of his ten injunctions, that Silla, one of the kingdoms he defeated, fell because too many influential people had built too many temples wherever they wished? Or, pursuing the theme of the relationship between human beings and the natural world into poetry, what issues does the repeated theme of rustic retirement in Korean poetry engage? Why do so many scholar-officials seem to be dying for a week or a month or a lifetime in the country?

The first part of this book is an anthology of texts "representative" in, I hope, several ways. First, they represent genres of Korean writing and the figures associated with them. The texts are also a series of engagements with recurrent themes or issues in Korean cultural history, one of which is the question of how Korea has represented itself. After studying these stories, legends, poems, historical vignettes, and other works, a reader curious about Korean literature may be able to respond in some way to the question, What is Korean literature like? And perhaps, What is Korea like? The translations are one answer.

My curiosity has also led me to write several essays over the years about how texts may be read as contracts. Written works summarize and inscribe previous and ongoing negotiations about subjects or events that may or may not appear in them; they ascribe meanings to events and names; they claim the authority to produce and to be a written record. How does a Korean historical work establish its authenticity and authority? Is the negotiation of textual authority comparable at all to negotiations of political authority, as for example when a new dynasty seeks to justify its usurpation of power from the previous one, or to quell the lingering resentments of those directly or indirectly affected by the change? How does a vernacular Korean verse form validate its existence as a text within a Sinocentric, "Chinese" literary and cultural realm? More broadly, how did Korea maintain and continue its cultural identity in confrontation with the hegemonic power and authority of the Chinese state and culture?

Such questions are the basis for the three chapters that comprise the second half of this volume and raise interpretive or comparative issues that may facilitate engagement with the selections in part 1. I hope the anthology and the essays will encourage further reading in other, more comprehensive collections, and I have listed some of the possibilities in the bibliography.

I wish to record my gratitude to a few out of the many who have inspired this project. First, my fond appreciation for the energetic, demanding Cornell undergraduates with whom it was my pleasure to study Korean literary and cultural history in "Introduction to Korea." Among many Cornell faculty colleagues who encouraged my efforts, I am especially grateful to Karen Brazell, Edward Gunn, Barry Strauss, and Gail Holst-Warhaft, and to Carol O'Brien, Director of the University Development Office during my years in Communications and Foundation Relations, for her understanding of my pursuits "up on the hill." Keith Taylor and I shared an office at Cornell where his enthusiastic antiestablishmentarianism and stories about amazing Michigan winters challenged my complacency and imagination. Robert Provine's patient questioning of my writing about the *Song of the Dragons* helped me avoid several pitfalls I had dug for myself. To Professor Edward Shultz at the University of Hawaii, for his help and suggestions, for presiding at the *Korean Studies* journal, and for his hospitality,

Mahalo. And the same to Jennifer Crewe, editor at Columbia University Press, for her unflappable encouragement.

To Korean scholars my indebtedness is immense, and can only be hinted at by my naming a few. The late Professor Chŏng Pyŏng-uk of Seoul National University cheered me, an eager but abashed graduate student, with conversation and beef soup, while the late Professor Pak Sŭng-ŭi of Korea University graciously permitted me to sit in on his seminar in traditional Korean literature, reading the *Samguk yusa.* I thank Professor Sin Dong-Wook, now of Kumamoto University in Japan, for his many years of friendly advice. Professor Kwŏn Young-min, of Seoul National University, and Mr. Yu Sang-duk, President of the Korean Education Research Council and former Vice President of the Korean Teachers Association, have been patient guides. Professor Peter H. Lee, now at UCLA, and his many pioneering works in the field of Korean literature have long been a model. Choong Nam Yoon, director of the Korean section at the Harvard Yenching Library, helped me many times with practical advice and suggestions. I owe a special debt to Professor Hŏ Kyŏng-jin of Mogwŏn University. When I asked for his guidance in making a selection of representative Chinese-language poems, he brought me forty of his books of translations into modern Korean, with suggestions marked. The natural, balanced flow of his translations established a pattern to try for in my own versions. I am especially grateful to Jiwon Shin, a graduate student at Harvard University, and to Dr. Ch'oi Kyŏng-hwan, Visiting Research Scholar at Harvard, for their critically alert and generous readings of the manuscript for this book.

My wife, Ann, requires a separate entry in this ledger. My true companion on these and all other journeys, she has always helped keep things in perspective, and has shared in my pleasure when a dragon does fly.

Most of all, I remember my friend and colleague Marshall Pihl. His advice, deeply informed, careful, and caring, helped keep me going during the decade and more when we each had found work as academic administrators. After many years of labor in those vineyards he journeyed to the University of Hawaii and helped to bring the American scholarly field of Korean literature to life. His students, colleagues, and many friends miss him—as I do.

I dedicate this book, sadly but gratefully, to his memory.

EARLY KOREAN LITERATURE

A BRIEF HISTORY OF KOREAN LITERATURE
TO THE NINETEENTH CENTURY

Prior to the twentieth century, Korean literature included works written in the Korean language and also, because of Korea's close political and cultural association with China and the plain usefulness of the medium, in Chinese. Prior to the fifteenth-century promulgation of the Korean alphabet, Korean literary works were recorded either in Chinese translation or in various systems of Chinese characters used to represent the meanings, sounds, and grammatical markings of Korean. Writing in Chinese stopped once at the end of the nineteenth century with the abolition of the state examination system, which had been based upon mastery of Chinese materials, and then again in 1919, in the surge of nationalist feeling that accompanied the March 1 Independence Movement. Since then, Korean literature has been written for the most part in the Korean language, although during the Japanese colonial occupation (1910–1945), especially the 1930s and early '40s, a significant body of literature by Koreans was published in Japanese. The famously modernist writer Yi Sang (1910–1937), for example, published much of his early work in the Japanese language. Ethnic enclaves in Russia, Manchuria, Japan, the United States, and elsewhere in the Korean diaspora have created works in other languages that speak for and to a Korean cultural identity. Because of restrictions on publishing in South Korea, from the 1950s until well into the 1980s the works of Korean writers and literary scholars who had "gone North" after the 1945 division of the country were not available in the South, yet still were assuredly "Korean."

EARLIEST WRITTEN REMAINS

There are few direct literary remains from before the establishment of the Unified Silla kingdom (668–918). The stone monument of King Kwanggaet'o (391–413) of Koguryŏ records the history and extent of his reign. Ancient songs like "Song of the Oriole" and stories such as that of Tan'gun, legendary founder of the Korean people whose tomb was recently discovered near P'yŏngyang in North Korea,[1] were first recorded in writings that have been lost, but were re-recorded in later works such as Kim Pu-sik's *Samguk sagi* (SGSG), *History of the Three Kingdoms* (1145), and the monk Iryŏn's *Samguk yusa* (SGYS), *Remnants of the Three Kingdoms* (1285). References by title to Koguryŏ (37 B.C.–668 A.D.) and Paekche (18 B.C.–663 A.D.) songs are included in the fifteenth-century *Koryŏ sa*, the *History of Koryŏ;* the text of one Paekche song is found in the *Akhak kwebŏm, Primer for Music Studies*, 1493. Various Silla (57 B.C.–918 A.D.) songs are recorded in the SGYS.

UNIFIED SILLA AND PAEKCHE

Silla narrative literature is represented in the SGYS; in the *Haedong kosŭng chŏn, Tales of Eminent Korean Monks* (1215); in quotations in the SGYS from the *Hwarang segi, Stories of the Hwarang Knights*, by Kim Tae-mun, eighth century; and in scattered references or entries in Chinese and Japanese works. The *Complete T'ang Poetry, Quan Tang shi*, 1705, includes works by several Silla poets, for example, while the eighth-century *Nihonshoki* refers to a Paekche man who taught Chinese-style *gigaku*, Buddhist ceremonial dance, in Japan.[2] One scholar has noted that the "most original voice" in the eighth-century Japanese anthology of poetry the *Man'yō shū*, Yamanoue no Okura (660–ca. 733), was of Paekche origins, though he had gone to Japan at the age of three and wrote very much as a "native son."[3]

The most noteworthy literary genre of Silla times are the songs called *hyangga*, or native songs. The fourteen *hyangga* in the SGYS range in subject matter from playful folk songs such as the "Song of Sŏdong," "*Sŏdonggyo*," and the "Flower Offering Song," "*Hŏnhwaka*," which suggest that folk songs were absorbed into the *hyangga* repertoire, to Buddhist devotional hymns and songs dedicated to exemplary *hwarang* knights. These *hyangga* are especially interesting because they were recorded using Chinese characters to represent the Korean language, rather than as Chinese translations. Reference to a now lost, ninth-century *hyangga* collection, the *Samdae mok*, or *Three-Epochs Collection*, in the SGSG suggests that the number of such works must have been substantial.

KORYŎ (918–1392)

While the Koryŏ period presents a substantial broadening and deepening of Korean literary genres, a multiplication of individual works and anthologies, and the emergence of writers like Yi Kyu-bo (1168–1241) who were concerned with matters of literary expression and form, this more detailed and varied picture of Koryŏ literature is also a measure of the survival of a greater number of works from the period.

Koryŏ instituted a state civil service examination in 958, patterned on the Chinese system, which used Chinese literary, philosophical, and historical sources and materials. One result of this official centering of Chinese materials was the importance of the Chinese *shi* and *fu*, poetry and rhyme-prose, in Korean literary compositions. Ch'oe Ch'ung (984–1068) and Kim Hwang-wŏn (1045–1117); Yi Kyu-bo and Chŏng Chi-sang (?–1135); and the Bamboo Grove Assembly, *Chungnim kohoe*, a group of seven highly regarded poets of the late twelfth century, are a few examples of Koryŏ poets who excelled in Chinese poetry genres.

The *hyangga* tradition continued into Koryŏ; the best known example is the series of eleven devotional hymns composed by the Buddhist monk Kyunyŏ (923–973).[4] The monk Chinul's (1128–1210) disciple Hyesim (1178–1234) wrote Chinese poems on *sŏn* (Zen) subjects and also collected Buddhist tales, meditation puzzles, allegories, and poems in a thirty-volume anthology, *Sŏnmun yŏmsong* (1226), or *Praise and Puzzle in Sŏn Literature*. The monk Ch'ungji (1226–1293) focused in his poetry upon the plight of the Korean people forced during the late thirteenth-century Mongol campaign against Japan to construct and man an invasion fleet.[5] References to other Buddhist monks are included in the *Haedong kosŭng chŏn* (1215), *Lives of Eminent Korean Monks*.[6]

Koryŏ literary genres of note included collections of fantastic stories, such as the *Sui chŏn,* ascribed to Ch'oe Ch'i-wŏn (857–951) in an original version that was lost, then republished in several later versions, also lost but from which several stories were finally gathered into other collections that have survived; long poems about Korean history, such as the "Poem for King Tongmyŏng," *"Tongmyŏngwang p'yŏn,"* by Yi Kyu-bo or the "Ode on Emperors and Kings," *"Chewang un'gi,"* (1287), by Yi Sung-hyu (1224–1300); "pseudo-biographies" such as the "Story of Mr. Yeast," *"Kuk sŏnsaeng chŏn,"* also by Yi Kyu-bo; biographies, autobiographies, and the *munjip,* collected writings, of literati such as Yi Il-lo (1152–1220), whose *P'ahan chip, Collection for Overcoming Leisure,* is cited as Korea's first collection of literary criticism.[7]

Notable among Koryŏ writings and literature were the mostly Chinese-language (with Korean-language refrains) *Kyŏnggi*-style songs, or *Kyŏnggich'e ka,* of which the *"Hallim pyŏlgok,"* "Song of the Capital" (thirteenth century) is the best known example. Koryŏ popular songs in Korean, *sogyo,* collected in the *Akchang kasa,* or *Words for Akchang* (sixteenth century), include *"Kasiri,"* "Would You Go?" and *"Ch'ŏngsan pyŏlgok,"* "Song of the Green Hills." Kim Pu-sik's (1075–1151) *Samguk sagi, History of the Three Kingdoms,* and the monk Iryŏn's (1206–1289) *Samguk yusa, Remnants of the Three Kingdoms,* a compilation from many sources of Korean legends, myths, histories, biographies, songs, and spells, are major landmarks in Korea's political, cultural, and literary history.

EARLY CHOSŎN (1392–1598)

The first two hundred years of the Chosŏn dynasty, from its founding in 1392 until the end of the disastrous invasions by the Japanese armies of Hideyoshi in 1598, was a period of great artistic creativity and cultural and scientific accomplishments. The new dynasty was only fifty years old when its fourth king, Sejong (r. 1418–1450), promulgated a new phonetic alphabet, now known as *han'gŭl,* for the Korean language. Composition in the Korean vernacular flourished, especially in two verse forms, the three-line *sijo* and the longer *kasa.* Many anthologies of Korean literature were assembled and published; numerous literary groups coalesced around various schools of literary thought, preferences for Chinese or Korean forms of expression, and not infrequently, political-philosophical outlooks. A brief survey of literary forms, subjects, and representative authors can do no more than suggest the scale of this literary realm.

Akchang was a verse form written for performance at state ceremonies. The two best known examples are both associated with King Sejong. The first, *Yongbi ŏch'ŏn ka* or *Song of the Dragons Flying to Heaven,* was composed, at Sejong's order, to praise the dynasty's founders. It was completed in 1445, in Chinese, then translated into Korean, annotated, and finally published two years later in an edition of 550 copies, distributed at court. Sejong himself is said to have written the other notable *akchang, Wŏrin ch'ŏn'gang chi kok* or *The Moonlight on Ten Thousand Waters,* published in 1449, as a remembrance of Queen Sohŏn, who had died in 1446.

The *sijo* is a Korean-language verse form composed for musical, sung performance. Its historical origins are obscured by the late development of the Korean alphabet, relative to the earliest examples of the genre, and by the fact that most of the *sijo* anthologies date from the eighteenth century or later. Chŏng Ch'ŏl (1536–1593) composed dozens, in addition to his four famous *kasa* poems. Some reflect his difficult political circumstances, others a more general philosophical outlook, and still others a directly didactic intent, as for example in the series written to instruct the people in the province where he had been sent as governor. Yi Hwang (1501–1570), one of the great Neo-Confucian philosophers of Chosŏn Korea, loved the song aspect of *sijo,* and the positive effect that singing and listening could have on both the performer/composer and the audience. The woodblocks carved from Yi's own calligraphy for his "Twelve Songs of Tosan" (1565) are the oldest of all *sijo* source materials.

The first example of the *kasa,* a Korean-language verse form of variable length, was Chŏng Kŭg-in's (1401–1481) "Song to Spring," "*Sangch'un kok,*" praising life in the countryside. Chŏng Ch'ŏl's four *kasa* employed a lyrical approach to composition, with each poem assembled from *sijo*-like units linked by a progression through time in the songs to the Beautiful One, *Miin gok,* or space in the travel poems, *pyŏlgok.* Hŏ Ch'o-hŭi (1563–1589), better known in Korea by her pen name, Nansŏrhŏn, wrote many highly regarded Chinese *shi,* as well as two *kasa,* "Married Sorrow," "*Kyuwŏn ka,*" and "The Touch-Me-Not," "*Pongsŏnhwa.*" Pak Il-lo (1561–1643) wrote quantities of didactic, philosophical *sijo,* and seven *kasa* of remarkably different, colloquial, narrative distinction. His "Song of Peace," "*T'aep'yŏng sa*" (1598), is a famous commemoration of the end of the Japanese invasions of Korea.

Writings in Chinese included the verse forms of *shi* and *fu*; theoretical and critical essays such as Sŏ Kŏ-jŏng's (1420–1488) "*Tongin sihwa,*" or "On Korean (Easterners') Poetry," which explored the relative merits of classical Chinese and Korean poetry in Chinese; and miscellanies such as Sŏ's *Great Peace Collection of Talk and Tales, T'aepyŏng hanhwa kŏlgye chŏn* (late fifteenth century), or O Suk-kwŏn's *P'aegwan chapki, Notes on Various Stories* (sixteenth century). Kim Si-sŭp's (1435–1493) ghost tales became popular in Japan as well as in Korea. *The Flower History, Hwa sa,* by Im Che (1549–1587) satirized the factional struggles of the day.

One characteristic feature of Korean literature is the grave seriousness of literary expression, one of the most famous examples of which is the *sijo* traditionally ascribed to the Koryŏ loyalist Chŏng Mong-ju (1337–1392). A government official known even in China as an accomplished statesman, Chŏng stymied the takeover being engineered by General Yi Sŏng-gye and his followers with his continued opposition. The story associated with Chŏng's famous *sijo* relates that the general's son, Pang-wŏn (1367–1422), organized a banquet, invited Chŏng, and then offered a somewhat mocking, metaphorical toast, couched in a *sijo* song, urging Chŏng to stop resisting the changing times. Chŏng's reply has become known as the "Song of a Loyal Heart," or "*Tansim ka*":

> Though this body die
>   and die and die again,
> white bones become but dust,
>   a soul exist, then not,
> Still, this single-hearted loyalty to my lord:
>   How could it waver, ever?

According to the story, Chŏng Mong-ju was assassinated soon after.[8] There is no mention of the banquet or the exchange of *sijo*, however, in the historical account of Chŏng's death found in the *History of Koryŏ.*

In 1456, in the aftermath of Sejo's (r. 1455–1468) usurpation of the throne and assassination of its occupant, his own nephew Tanjong (r.

1452–1455), Sŏng Sam-mun (1418–1456), one of the "Six Martyred Minis-ters" put to death for a plan to bring Tanjong back to the throne, composed a *sijo* on the eve of his execution that echoes Chŏng's:[9]

> Once this body is dead and gone
>   you ask, what will it be?
> On the highest peak of Pongnae Mountain
>   a towering, spreading pine.
> When sky and earth are filled with white snow,
>   alone and green, green, shall I be.

Less immediately threatening but still dangerous conditions, such as the endemic factional struggles and political purges that brought various groups into ascendancy or decline, seem to have inspired *sijo* and *kasa* praising famous places away from the capital and the life of rustic seclu-sion. Yi Hwang's (1501–1570) "Twelve Songs of Tosan," "*Tosan sibi kok*," Yi I's (1536–1584) "Nine Songs from Kosan," "*Kosan kugok ka*," and the "Song of Myŏnang Pavilion," "*Myŏnang chŏng ka*," by Song Sun (1493–1583) convey a note of political complaint at exile. Chŏng Ch'ŏl's two famous travel poems, "Song of Sŏng Mountain," "*Sŏngsan pyŏlgok*," and "Song of Kwandong," "*Kwandong pyŏlgok*," offer a more exuberant than downcast view of the Korean landscape, while Chŏng's two other *kasa*, "Longing for the Beautiful One," "*Samiin kok*," and "Again, Beautiful One," "*Sok miin kok*," are read as expressions, in the dramatic persona of a woman abandoned, of Chŏng's own resentment at being dismissed from office and sent into exile.

LATER CHOSŎN

Between the end of the Japanese invasions in 1598 and the end of the dynasty itself in 1910, vernacular genres, especially the verse-drama known as *p'ansori*, brought literary expression into the lives of the broad-est possible spectrum of Koreans, from upper-class *yangban* officials in their stately surroundings to anyone who came to a village on market day. As literature spread throughout society, its philosophical framework shifted dramatically in both Korean vernacular and Chinese-language forms, from idealized character types, settings, or subjects to real-life situations, observations of actual places in Korea, and engagements with contemporary issues. The philosophical movement known as *sirhak*, or practical learning, swept up not just philosophy but literature, painting, and the sciences as well. Had Western systems of thought, with their powerful political and economic underpinnings, not come to Korea in the late nineteenth century, followed by the shock of Japanese neocolonial aggression in the early twentieth, it is arguable that modern Korean literature would have evolved directly from its own eighteenth-century beginnings. The Japanese colonial occupation (1910–1945), the foreign military occupation (1945–1948), and the restrictive political regimes in the North and South, a divided Korea, further bent the growth of Korean literature until the final decades of the twentieth century.

Four writers and their works may be seen as illustrating the breadth of seventeenth-century Korean literature. The life of the poet Pak Il-lo (1561–1643) bridges two centuries almost equally. His "Song of Peace," mentioned above, marked the close of the sixteenth century's final devastating decade. While his *sijo* verse compositions are but dull expressions of Confucian precepts, his *kasa* are another matter entirely. The "Lament on the Waters," "*Sŏnsangt'ang*" (1605), returns to the theme of the naval campaign against the Japanese. "The Sedge Bank," "*Saje kok*" (1611), is a portrait of a rural retreat. "Song of a Humble Life," "*Nuhang sa*" (1611), combines realistic plot, vividly observed setting, and strikingly "modern," vernacular dialogue in a unique expression of a traditional theme.

Hŏ Kyun (1569–1618), brother of Hŏ Nansŏrhŏn, mentioned above, is generally thought to have written the *Tale of Hong Kil-tong, Hong Kil-tong chŏn* (date uncertain), as a literary protest of the state's discriminatory laws against secondary sons, that is, the sons of secondary wives or concubines. The eponymous hero of the story, a secondary son, is forced from his upper-class home into a Robin Hood-like outlaw existence. Hŏ Kyun was tried and executed for his inadvertent association with a wretchedly conceived protest plot by a group of *sŏja*, secondary sons. Kim Man-jung (1637–1692) wrote *The Nine-Cloud Dream, Kuun mong* (1687–1688), a Buddhist fantasy set in T'ang China, supposedly to console his mother during his sentence in exile. Though both works seem limited by unrealistic characters and antirealist settings and plots, the melancholy nature of the stories is a poignant reminder of the circumstances in which they were written. That poignancy and the claim, though it is difficult to substantiate, that both were originally written in the Korean language have given the works a solid position in the Korean national literary pantheon.

Yun Sŏn-do (1587–1671) was a brilliant innovator in the *sijo* form, and wrote numerous individual works and *sijo* sequences. The most famous of the latter is his *Fisherman's Calendar, Ŏbu sasi sa* (1651), a four-part, forty-poem sequence on the pleasures of the fisherman's tranquil existence. These poems are notable for their clear and flowing vernacular diction, their use of an onomatopoeic refrain, and the deliberately controlled relaxation of the usual structural patterns of the *sijo*.

For all of its meticulous insistence on actual observation for scientific studies, close attention to the circumstances of ordinary Korean life in literature, and careful observation of the Korean landscape, the *sirhak* movement did not entail any ideological stand against the use of the Chinese language. Several of the better known writers of the eighteenth century illustrate the point. Hong Tae-yong (1731–1783) and Pak Chi-wŏn (1737–1805) wrote in Chinese of travels to China and of the changes taking place there under the influence of Western science and technology. Both wrote travel journals and snapshotlike *hansi*, Chinese poems, about life in rural Korea. Pak's "The Story of Master Hŏ," "*Hŏsaeng chŏn,*" from his China travel diary *Yŏrha ilgi* (1780), presents a sustained analysis of Korea's political-economic circumstances in sharply drawn satire. Four poets known as the "Four Masters" were admired in China as well as Korea for their innovative *hansi* and attention to Korean life: Yi Tŏng-mu (1741–1793), Yu Tŭk-kong (1749–1807), Pak Che-ga (1750–1805), and Yi Sŏ-gu (1754–1825). They, along with Pak Chi-wŏn and Hong Tae-yong, brought Korean literature in Chinese to a widely acknowledged high point.[10]

P'ansori is a form of spoken and sung dramatic performance in which a singer, the *kwangdae,* accompanied only by a drummer, recites a long narrative. Of twelve known stories, five survive in performance: the *Song of Ch'unhyang, Ch'unhyang ka;* the *Song of Sim Ch'ŏng, Simch'ŏng ka;* the *Song of Hŭngbu, Hŭngbu ka;* the *Song of the Water Palace, Sugung ka;* and the *Song of Red Cliffs, Chŏkpyŏk ka.* The original style of performance in *p'ansori* is thought to have developed in Chŏlla Province from dramatic narrative associated with shamanistic ceremonies; it reached the apogee of its popularity in the nineteenth century. Sin Chae-hyo's (1812–1884) lifework of writing down the *p'ansori* scripts and recording its histories and techniques preserved an important part of the heritage, as did the many so-called "*p'ansori* novels," which adapted the stories to a marketable book form during the nineteenth century. With other dramatic forms such as the various regional puppet plays and mask dances, *p'ansori* went into decline in the early twentieth century, in part because of Western drama's popular impact.[11] Though these forms of dramatic performance have been studied and revived recently, notably through state-supported cultural programs and, ironically in that context, student political protests, several generations of the tradition were lost.

Court memoirs, written in Korean by women at court, are an additional trove of prose work that has only recently been given much sustained attention. Two examples are the anonymous *Tale of Queen Inhyŏn, Inhyŏn wanghu chŏn,* about the life of Queen Inhyŏn (1667–1701), and the *Record in Sorrow, Hanjung nok,* written as four separate memoirs by Lady Hong (1735–1815), widow of the Korean crown prince, during the final years of her life. Lady Hong's painful story tries to explain the circumstances of the death of her husband at the command of his father the king.[12]

The nineteenth century has been viewed as the nether end of a long but declining tradition. *P'ansori* flared up, then was extinguished; *sijo* and *kasa* continued to be performed and composed, though without notable accomplishment. Prose lost the vigor of earlier examples, and then was replaced by Western forms. Korean literature written in Chinese faded, ultimately to be extinguished as a literary medium with the abolition, in 1894, of the state examination system.

An alternative view would describe the nineteenth century as a continuation of the experiments with forms, voices, media, and subjects that began in the eighteenth century and before. This view leads me to end the present collection of readings in traditional Korean literature with Pak Chi-wŏn's "Story of Master Hŏ." The project will continue with a second volume on eighteenth- and nineteenth-century Korean literature.

PART I

An Anthology of Korean Literature

THE *SAMGUK SAGI* (1145)

The *Samguk sagi, History of the Three Kingdoms*—Silla, Paekche, and Koguryŏ—was written at royal request by Kim Pu-sik (1075–1151). The *sagi* was modeled on the dynastic histories of China, which meant, among other things, that it was organized into sections such as history, biographies, and notable events; it tended to present the state officials as the principle actors; and, of course, it was written in literary Chinese, the same literary language as was used in China for such records.

Kim Pu-sik enjoyed a high reputation as a government officer, historian, and writer. (One of his poems is included in the Chinese poetry section of this anthology.) He and his work have suffered at the hands and minds of modern historians, however, who find too much deference to China in his approach to the history project.

"Song of the Oriole"

In October of that winter, Queen Song passed away. The king, Yuri, found two women and took them into his service. One of them, the royal concubine Hwa, was the daughter of someone from Kolch'ŏn, while the other, Ch'i, was the daughter of a Han (Chinese) man. The two were jealous, and relations between them were not good.

It happened that the king went out to Kisan and for some time did not return. The jealous feelings between the two did not improve in the interval. At one point, in her anger, Concubine Hwa taunted Ch'i, saying "You are nothing but a Han house slave turned concubine. That's all you are!" Ch'i was mortified. Unable to bear the resentment she felt, she returned to her home.

The king heard of this and tried to get her to change her mind, but Ch'i could not forget her sense of humiliation and did not return.

The king happened to be resting by a tree and noticed the orioles fluttering around each other affectionately. He composed a song about his feelings. The song was as follows:

> Fluttering, the orioles
> male and female together, so.
> Reminded of my loneliness;
> with whom will I ever go?

THE *SAMGUK YUSA* (1285)

The *Samguk yusa, Remnants of the Three Kingdoms,* was compiled over a period of several years by the Buddhist monk Iryŏn (1206–1289). Quite deliberately assembled as a supplement to Kim Pu-sik's *Samguk sagi,* the *yusa* draws together a wide assortment of myths, legends, genealogies, histories, Buddhist tales, observations by the compiler, and other materials. Of key significance among these, fourteen *hyangga,* native songs, are transcribed as Korean-language texts, using Chinese characters to convey meanings, sounds, and grammatical inflections, embedded in the literary Chinese narrative. In the following stories, "The Flower Offering Song" in "Suro," Ch'ŏyong's song, and Sŏdong's in "King Mu" are all examples of *hyangga.* Additional song texts in the *yusa* such as the sea spirit song in the story of Lady Suro, like the "Song of the Oriole" from the *Samguk sagi,* were recorded in Chinese translations.

The *yusa* of the title—"remaining matters," or "miscellany"—can be read as a reference to Kim Pu-sik's work, meaning those historical details and oral, vernacular materials that the earlier work omitted. The phrase might also be read as making a contemporaneous, thirteenth-century reference to Korea's precarious situation following the devastating Mongol invasions that began in 1231 and ended in 1259.

Book 1: Tan'gun (*Ancient Chosŏn*)

In the *Wei shu* there is the following. Two thousand years ago, Tan'gun Wanggŏm, selecting Asadal as the capital—in the classics also referred to as Muyŏpsan, or as Paegak, in Paekchu; also said to be east of Kaesŏng, but right where present-day Paegakkung is located—founded the nation. He named it Chosŏn. This was in the time of Yao.

In the Old Record there is the following. In ancient times, Hwanung, the son of Hwanin, set his mind constantly on the human world, wishing to bring order to human life. Knowing his son's intentions, the father went to Samwi T'aebaek Mountain, deciding this location would be the most advantageous for human affairs. He gave his son three heavenly seals, telling him to go down and take charge of human affairs.

With three thousand attendants, Hwanung descended to a place below the holy altar tree on the peak of Mount T'aebaek, now known as Mount Myohyang. He named this place City of God, did Hwanung the heavenly king. He led the Earl of Wind, the Master of Clouds, and the Master of Rain, and allocating the three hundred areas of governance according to the categories of agriculture, existence, illness, law, and morals, he domesticated human affairs.

At that time a bear and a tiger were living in a cave. They prayed constantly to Hwanung to be turned into humans. At last he gave them a wick of wormwood and twenty garlic cloves and told them, "If you eat these and for one hundred days avoid the light of the sun, you will become human."

The bear and tiger took them and ate. The bear, after twenty-one days of avoiding the sun, turned into a human, but the tiger could not avoid it and failed to become human. The bear that had become a human could not find a mate, and so by the holy altar tree prayed to become pregnant. Hwanung thereupon changed for a while into human form, and joined her in marriage. She became pregnant and gave birth to a son. He was named Tan'gun Wanggŏm.

In the year of Kyŏngin, the fiftieth year of the reign of the Yao king—though because it is not certain what the foundation year of Yao was, it is not entirely certain that it was the fiftieth year—Wanggŏm moved the capital to P'yŏngyang—present-day Sŏgyŏng—and, as noted, named the country Chosŏn. Then he moved the capital again, to Asadal at Paegak

Mountain. The place is also called Kŭmmidal, as well as Kungholsan, according to the region. He ruled the land for 1,500 years. In the Kimyo year, when King Wu of Chou enfeoffed Kija with Chosŏn, Tan'gun moved to Changdan'gyŏng. However, he returned later and hid at Asadal as the mountain god. He was said to be 1,908 years old.

In the T'ang book of Paegu there is the following. Koguryŏ was originally known as Kojuk—present-day Haeju—but when Kija was enfeoffed, it became known as Chosŏn. The Han state divided this into three administrative districts, Hyŏndo, Nangnang, and Taebang, the Northern Belt.

Book 2: The Story of Lady Suro

In the time of King Sŏngdŏk, Lord Sunjŏng was making his way as *T'aesu*—now *Myŏngju*—to take office in Kangnŭng. He stopped for a meal by the seashore. The tops of the cliffs extended there like a folding screen facing the sea. The heights seemed to reach the heavens, where royal azaleas blossomed in magnificent glory.

His lordship's wife, Suro, as she looked at the sight, said to her attendants, "Would someone go and pick those flowers for me?" They answered, "That is a place where no human feet can go." They all said it could not be done.

Just then an old fellow passing by with a cow heard the lady's words. He picked the flowers and brought them, offering them with a song. No one knew what kind of person the old fellow was.

They went on, reaching Imhae, or Facing the Sea, Pavilion. As they paused for a meal, suddenly a dragon came up from the sea, seized Lady Suro, and disappeared into the waters. Lord Sunjŏng flung himself down to the ground, with no idea what to do. Another old fellow was there and said, "The people of old used to say that the voices of many together will melt something even as hard as iron. Just so, will that sea creature not dread the voices of these many people? Assuredly, all the people of the district must be gathered together. Then if a song is composed and sung and the hilltops are pounded with great staves, the lady can be found again."

Lord Sunjŏng followed these directions, and the dragon lifted up Lady Suro, came out of the sea, and returned her.

When Lord Sunjŏng asked her about things beneath the sea, Lady Suro replied, "The food in the palace decorated with seven different kinds of treasures, it was so sweet and fragrant. It is unlike any human food."

From her clothes there came a strange, unearthly fragrance.

Lady Suro was an incomparable beauty. Even deep in the mountains, whenever she passed near a body of water, the water spirits would always come and carry her away.

The words that the many people chanted in their sea song were as follows:

Sea spirit, sea spirit, let Lady Suro go.
How great the crime, to take another's wife.
If you refuse to give her back,
we will go into the water to catch you, and cook you, and
    eat you.

The old fellow's song of offering the flowers was as follows:

By the deep-red rocks
letting the cow go,
If you will not be shy of me
may I pluck the flowers and have you take them?

Book 2: Ch'ŏyong and Manghae Temple

In the time of Hŏn'gang, the forty-ninth king, in the capital and all the land within the seas, the walls of the houses touched, and there was not a single thatched roof. Piping and songs were constant along the roadways, and the wind and rains were in harmony with the four seasons.

The king had gone out to Kaeunp'o, in the southwestern part of Haksŏng, now called Ulju, and had turned his carriage to return. As he ordered a rest beside the shore, clouds and fog suddenly obscured and darkened the way. They lost the road. The king asked his retinue what had happened, and the soothsayer said that it was the changing of the dragon of the Eastern Sea and that it would clear away if an appropriate thing were done.

The king thereupon issued a royal command that a Buddhist temple be built for the dragon near the border. As soon as the command went forth, the clouds broke up and the fog scattered. Therefore the place is called Kaeunp'o, Port of Opening Clouds.

The dragon of the Eastern Sea was pleased, and appeared by the royal carriage with his seven sons. Praising the king's virtues, they offered dances and music.

One of the sons accompanied the royal carriage back to the capital, to assist with the administration. His name was Ch'ŏyong. The king gave him a beautiful woman as his wife, and bestowed upon him the office of *Kŭpkan*, so as to retain his loyal intentions.

The wife's beauty was such that the Demon Spirit came to adore her. Changing into human form, it came at night to the house and secretly joined her where she was sleeping.

Ch'ŏyong came back to the house from outside, and saw two people there. He thereupon sang a song, made a dance, and withdrew. The song went as follows:

> In the bright moon of the capital
> I enjoyed the night until late.
> When I came back and looked in my bed
> there were four legs in it.
> Two are mine,
> but the other two—Whose are they?

Once upon a time that was mine;
what shall be done, now these are taken?

Then the spirit appeared in its own form. Kneeling before him, it said: "I desired your wife, and now I have despoiled her. But because you did not show anger, I am moved by your action and see it as beautiful. I swear that from now on, if I so much as see a likeness of yourself, I shall not enter the gate."

Owing to this, the people of this country make gate plates with Ch'ŏyong's likeness. In this way, misfortune is kept at a distance and happiness drawn near.

After the king returned, he chose a place on the eastern side of Yŏngch'u (Spirit Eagle) Mountain where he had a temple constructed. The temple was called Manghaesa, Sea View Temple, and also Sinbangsa, The New Temple. It was established for the dragon.

The king went out again, to P'osŏkchŏng. The spirit of South Mountain appeared and danced before the ruler. The attendants did not see it; only the king was able to see it, as a person who had appeared, dancing before him. The king himself performed the dance in order to demonstrate its form.

The spirit's name was Sangsim, Fortunate Manifestation. From that day until now, the people of this country have passed on this dance, calling it Ŏmu Sangsim, the Reign Dance for Sangsim. It is also called the Reign Dance for Sansin, the Mountain Spirit.

Furthermore, following the spirit's appearance in a dance and the king's examination of the basic forms of its manifestation, he ordered that it be carved in stone and thereby taught to succeeding generations. It was therefore proclaimed as Form Examination, and was also known as the Frosty Beard Dance. In this way its form praises the spirit.

At the time when the king went to Diamond Pass, Kŭmgangnyŏng, the spirit of the northern hills appeared and danced. It was called Ŏkdo-gŏm, Jade Blade Clasp.

Again, as the same ceremony was being held at a palace banquet, the earth spirit came forth and danced. It was called Kŭpkan of the Earth Elder.

According to an old book, at another time the mountain spirit presented a dance and sang a song that went: *chi ri da do p'a do p'a*. This meant: "Those who rule the country with wisdom understand and flee in great numbers." This was a revelation that the capital and districts were doomed. The earth spirit and the mountain spirit knew that the kingdom would be ruined, and for that reason made the dance to serve as a warning. The people of the country did not realize this but took the warning as a happy omen, and let their pleasures and enjoyment go from plentiful to extreme. For this reason, the kingdom ended in ruin.

Book 2: King Mu

In the old books it says (King) Mugang, but this is a mistake. There was no King Mugang in Paekche.

The name of the thirtieth ruler, King Mu, was Chang. His mother was a widow. She had built a house near a pond south of the capital. She had relations with the dragon of the pond, and gave birth to a son. His name was Sŏdong. His skills and talents were so many, it is impossible to count them. Probably because he made his living cultivating and selling yams, the people of that region called him Yam Boy, Sŏdong.

Hearing that Sŏnhwa, whose name is also written with the characters for *beautification*, the third daughter of King Chinp'yŏng of Silla, was a peerless beauty, Sŏdong cut his hair short and traveled to the Silla capital. There he gave the children of the region yams to eat, so they came to feel friendly toward him and follow him around. He then composed a song and taught them to sing it. The song was as follows:

> Princess Sŏnhwa keeps
> her secret love secret.
> She goes at night to sleep
> in the arms of her Sŏdong.

Before long, the song was heard everywhere in the capital. When the court officials reported this to the king, he ordered the princess into exile. Just as she was leaving, the queen gave her a quantity of gold for her travels.

As the princess was reaching the outskirts of town, Sŏdong appeared and, with a bow, announced that he wished to help her. For her part, though she had no real idea where he had come from, she quickly came to trust him. And so it was that as she went along with him, they formed a relationship. Afterward, when she learned his name at last, she realized the effects of the children's song.

After they arrived in Paekche, she uncovered the gold her mother had given her, saying it would be useful for their livelihood. Sŏdong laughed at this, saying "What is this stuff, then?" The princess replied, "It is gold. This much will enable us to have a prosperous life." "Since I was young," came the reply, "I piled up lots of this stuff like dirt, when I was digging my yams." Sŏnhwa, in astonishment, replied, "That is the most precious material under heaven. If you still know where it is, what would you think about sending an amount of it to my parents in the palace?"

Sŏdong agreed. He collected the gold, mounding it up like a hill. He asked the priest at Saja Temple what to do next. The priest replied, "Bring it to me. I can send it with my magical powers."

Sŏnhwa wrote a letter and brought it with the gold to Saja Temple. In one night, the priest sent it all to the Silla palace. King Chinp'yŏng regarded all this as quite miraculous. Holding Sŏdong in ever higher regard, he sent letters daily with his regards and greetings. Sŏdong consequently rose in the esteem of the people, and soon became king.

One day, King Mu and his wife were on their way to Saja Temple. As they reached the shore of a pond at the base of Mount Yonghwa, Dragon-Gleaming Mountain, an image of the Maitreya, Mirŭk, appeared in the midst of the waters. They stopped and offered obeisance on the spot. The queen said to the king, "We must build a great temple here. This is my earnest wish."

The king agreed. He went to the priest and asked about moving the pond. With his magical powers, in the space of one night the priest moved the pond and the mountain, and turned all into level ground. He fashioned a statue of the three-figured Maitreya. With the meditation hall, the pagoda, and the living quarters in their several places, the temple was named Mirŭk Temple. In the national history it is called Wanghŭng Temple, Temple of the King's Pleasure. King Chinp'yŏng sent many different kinds of laborers to assist with the construction. The temple still stands today.

In the *Three Kingdoms Chronicle*, he (Sŏdong) is referred to as the son of King Pŏp, while here as a widowed woman's son. There is no way to decide between the two accounts.

KORYŎ SONGS

Texts for "Would You Go?" and "Song of Green Mountains" are included in the sixteenth-century *Akchang kasa, Akchang Texts*. It has been pointed out that "Song of Green Mountains" can be read in at least two different ways: as the lament of people forced by hard times to scavenge for food, and as a cheerful song of upper-class enjoyment of the rustic life.

"Would You Go?", "*Kasiri*," is a prototypical folk song of parting. It is seen as a thematic precursor to the well-known folk song "Arirang," as well as the famous modern poem "Azaleas," "*Chindallaekkot*," by the poet Sowŏl, Kim Chŏng-sik (1902–1934).

Would You Go?

Anonymous

Would you go, would you go, would you?
Would you just go and leave me?

Oh what a time of great peace.

Then how, oh how shall I live
if you just go and leave me?

Oh what a time of great peace.

Though I might try to hold you,
still, if you are sad, might you return?

Oh what a time of great peace.

Though I must send you away,
why don't you just come back and stay?

Oh what a time of great peace.

Song of Green Mountains

I shall live, I shall live I say,
    I shall live in the green mountains.
I shall eat wild grapes and berries
    and live, I say, in the green mountains.

    Yalli yalli yallangsŏng, yallari yalla.

Cry, cry, O bird!
    Sleep to wake and cry, O bird.
With more cares than you,
    I sleep, to wake and cry.

    Yalli yalli yallasŏng, yallari yalla.

Did you see the bird that flew away?*
    Did you see the bird that flew off to the east?
Taking the old rusty plough,
    did you see that bird that flew off to the east?

    Yalli yalli yallasŏng, yallari yalla.

Doing this and doing that,
    and now the day has gone by.
With no one who comes and no one who goes,
    what shall I do to get through the night?

    Yalli yalli yallasŏng, yallari yalla.

Where was the stone thrown,
    who was it meant for?
With no one to hate, no one to regret,
    I was hit and I cry.

---

*A variant reading of the line takes it as "the ploughed field": Do you see the fields I once ploughed?

Yalli yalli yallasŏng, yallari yalla.

I shall live, I shall live I say,
    I shall live by the sea.
I shall eat oysters and clams and the seaweeds
    and live, I say, by the sea.

Yalli yalli yallasŏng, yallari yalla.

I shall go, I shall go and listen;
    I shall pass the last cooking place and listen.
Where the deer has climbed the bamboo pole,
    I shall listen as it plays the *haegŭm.**

Yalli yalli yallasŏng, yallari yalla.

Where I go, there in a fat jar
    the young wine is brewing.
When the strong smell of yeast cakes
    shaped like gourd flowers seizes me,
    what shall I do then?

Yalli yalli yallasŏng, yallari yalla.

*Haegŭm: A fiddle.

HISTORY AS LITERATURE:
THE POLITICAL AND CULTURAL
TRANSITION FROM KORYŎ TO CHOSŎN

Late Koryŏ and early Chosŏn, the inglorious end of one dynasty and the brutal beginning of the next, as even the brief summary below, in Book 2 of the Koryŏsa, suggests, was a fiercely contested period, historically and historiographically. The new rulers and especially the fourth king, Sejong, undertook many works to establish the foundations for a long-lasting dynasty. Legal reforms, re-siting the capital, development of agricultural technology, and a new alphabet were just a few of the elements in the program.

This section contains three examples of the struggle over history and historical culture, chosen to illustrate this transition period as one of forces contending not only in the political arena but also in the cultural and literary realms. The literary contestation begins with the famous *sijo* exchange between Yi Pang-wŏn, the dynasty founder's fifth son (by a second wife), who eventually became its third king, and Chŏng Mong-ju, a highly regarded Koryŏ loyalist. The exchange shows, as do the stories in the *Samguk yusa*, the significant role that songs and poetry have played in Korean political history. The exchange illustrates the penchant in Korean literary history for connecting historical anecdote to lyric song, as if to legitimize the vernacular, emotional expression with a more formal setting. The exchange also points to the problems in literary history posed by the facts that the Korean alphabet was not developed until the mid-fifteenth century; no historical record reflects the exchange or includes the texts; and *sijo* and other vernacular forms were not collected until the eighteenth-century anthologies assembled by Kim Su-jang and Kim Ch'ŏn-t'aek. In a technical sense, then, the stories that accompany most *sijo*, including the one attributed to Chŏng Mong-ju, are apocryphal. Another way to acknowledge the same point, however, is to note that the oral tradition includes both the song and the story in its telling and reciting, whereas the written records divide them. The recapturing of the oral vernacular record, we might remind ourselves, was one part of Iryŏn's purpose in assembling the *Samguk yusa*.

The *History of Koryŏ, Koryŏsa*, reflects another aspect of the transition. Compiled by the successor, Chosŏn dynasty, completed at about the same time as the promulgation of the Korean alphabet, and assembled by the same group of scholars who had worked on the dynastic hymn, the *Song of the Dragons Flying to Heaven*, the *History* has a distinctly programmatic air to it. The narrative movement—from the account of Wang Kŏn's founding of Koryŏ to the lugubrious, painful, embarrassing foolishness, corruption, and collapse of the final monarchs, including a brief flurry of monk's sons occupying the throne—argues implicitly that the Yi family's rise to ascendancy was called for by events. The account of Chŏng Mong-ju's murder at the hand of Pang-wŏn seems crafted almost as a legal brief, first to exculpate the dynastic founder Yi Sŏng-gye, then to demonstrate that the murder was carried out because of Pang-wŏn's filial fears for his father's life. Yi Sŏng-gye's final comment about the people of Korea suggests the hope that they will form their opinions about the new dynasty and its leaders on the basis of historical facts as presented in the *Koryŏsa* account, rather than the rumors about which he expresses such alarm.

The *Koryŏsa* is more than just a plain, narrative history; it raises questions about the very nature of historical writing. On the *Koryŏsa* model, history is propaganda. It is also literary. The passage in which Wang Kŏn announces the ten injunctions and dies soon after is elegantly crafted, and Wang Kŏn's final smile provides an artful conclusion. That scene was in turn ably rendered in the famous North Korean translation from literary Chinese into modern Korean published originally in P'yŏngyang in 1962, and republished, following the easing of political restrictions in South Korea, in 1991. The motif of a great leader's smile can also be seen in depictions of the late North Korean leader Kim Il Sung, who in all scenes of providing on-the-spot guidance was shown with a warm smile on his face.

The third selection in this section on dynastic transition, the royal ode *Yongbi ŏch'ŏn ka, Song of the Dragons Flying to Heaven*, is discussed at length in the second part of this book. Here let it be noted only that the song represented the first official, public use of the new Korean alphabet;

it constantly reiterated the parallel and yet distinct Korean and Chinese cultural/political histories and identities; and it engaged the vexing problem of old loyalties and resentments that always attended significant shifts in political alignments.

THE *SIJO* EXCHANGE BETWEEN
YI PANG-WŎN AND CHŎNG MONG-JU

The following *sijo* exchange is said to have taken place between Yi Pang-wŏn (1367–1422), fifth son of Yi Sŏng-gye, founder of the Chosŏn Dynasty, and Chŏng Mong-ju (1337–1392), Koryŏ statesman and loyalist. (The numbers following the names are the entry numbers for these *sijo* texts in Ch'ŏng Pyŏng-uk's *Sijo munhak sajŏn*. See the Notes for publication details.)

Things go this way, like them or not;
    things go that way too.
What if the vines on Mansu Mountain
    grow tangled and long? What of that?
Let us unwind just like them
    and enjoy life a hundred years more.

Yi Pang-wŏn (1641)

Though this body die
    and die and die again,
White bones become but dust,
    a soul exist, then not,
Still this single-hearted loyalty to my lord:
    how could it waver, ever?

Chŏng Mong-ju (1666)

THE *KORYŎSA: THE HISTORY OF KORYŎ*

Book 2: The Ten Injunctions and the Death of Wang Kŏn

In summer, the fourth month, in the twenty-sixth year of his reign, the king summoned Minister Pak Sul-hŭi and presented him with a set of injunctions, instructing him as follows.

According to what I have heard, when Shun was cultivating the field at Yŏksan, he nevertheless inherited the kingdom from Yao; and although Emperor Ko Cho (Ko Tsu) was born in humble circumstances, he founded the empire. I too come from modest origins, a house quite without connections, and yet, with undeserved support for my leadership, neither avoiding the heat of summer nor shunning the cold of winter, dedicating mind and body to the task for some nineteen years, I unified the three Han (kingdoms), and have ruled for more than twenty-five years. But now I have grown old. I worry that those who succeed me will succumb to their passions and forget their discipline. This is a matter of great concern. I have therefore drawn up the following injunctions. They should be studied morning to night, and now and ever after used as a mirror for contemplation.

First, all the accomplishments of our country are due to the energy received through the many instances of the Blessed Buddha's favor and protection. For this reason, temples of both the Meditation and Doctrinal schools should be established, and priests appointed to burn incense and conduct practice. Each part of this undertaking must be supervised carefully. It may happen that in later ages, corrupt officials may try to gain political power by acceding to the requests of the monks, setting one temple against another and stealing their domains. This must be prohibited.

Second, the new temples were all established in accordance with the decisions of the monk Tosŏn, who chose places that would have a favorable geomantic effect and confound the rebellious. Tosŏn said, if temples were built at random rather than in places that he selected, the virtuous strength of the land would become dissipated and the long life of the kingdom would be jeopardized. When we give thought to this, we are concerned that later generations of the royal house or officials or the leading families may very well desire to build prayer halls. But the end of the Silla kingdom serves as a lesson. Toward the end of that dynasty, many temples were built in a competitive striving for advantage, but as a result, the virtuous strength of the land was dissipated, and the state came to ruin.

Third, regarding the matter of the royal succession, it is well-established practice that the eldest son will succeed to the kingdom and the royal line. But in the case of ancient Yao in China, the succession passed to Shun instead, because the next in line of the Yao house was deemed unworthy. This was truly an example of having the public interest at heart. If the eldest son is seen to be unsuitable, then let this throne pass to the next son. If that son too should prove unsuitable, then have the throne pass to the son considered by the various ministers to be most suitable. In this way, the royal line can be continued.

Fourth, from ages past our people have modeled culture and ceremonies on those of T'ang. But the two lands are different, and the peoples are also different. Do not be obsequious, trying to copy things exactly. The Khitan, who rule the land next to us, are nothing but a country of animals. The dress and institutions of such as they must never be taken as models.

Fifth, our task of uniting the three Han kingdoms was achieved with the help of the beneficial effect of the terrain. The western capital, favored by the virtues of the waters, acts as a foundation for the rocky veins of our land. A royal visit must therefore be made four times each year, without fail, during the mid-month of each season. Stay a total of at least one hundred days, and in this way secure the well-being of the kingdom.

Sixth, the Lamp-lighting Festival is meant to honor Buddha, while the Festival of the Eight Gates is to honor the god of the heavens, the five mountain peaks and other mountains, the great streams, and the dragon spirit. It may happen that in later ages, corrupt officials may try to modify our practice, but this must be prohibited.

Seventh, it is extremely difficult for the king to win the trust of the officials and the common people. In order to earn their trust, pay heed to criticism that is sincere, and avoid slanderers. Though it may be sweet as honey to hear others being reviled, pay it no heed; it will die away by itself. Furthermore, if corvée labor is relatively light and adjusted to the appropriate season, if the burden of taxes is reasonable, and if effort is made to understand the real difficulties of the farmer's life, then the trust of the people will be gained, the prosperity of the country will be assured, and peace will rule among the common people. The Ancients had the following saying: "A fish will surely rise to a tasty-smelling bait; splendid generals will surely appear where generous rewards are given; birds will surely flee the drawn bow; the people will surely be virtuous where benevolence is bestowed upon them." If rewards and punishments are reasonable, then the yin and yang will remain in balance.

Eighth, in the territory south of the Ch'aryǒng Mountains and beyond the Kongju River, the shapes of the mountain ranges and the features of the terrain are disordered. The character of the people of that place is likewise disordered. If they should manage to work their way into government or marry into the royal family and seize political office, they will bring turmoil and disaster to the country. Or in their continuing resentment at Paekche's incorporation into the unified kingdom, they might demonstrate their feelings and cause disturbances along the routes of the royal processions. Furthermore, there will always be slaves, or servants assigned to government facilities or such, who will try to place themselves under the protection of certain powerful individuals and avoid their proper service, just as there will be those who, attaching themselves to members of the royal family or officers of government, with their clever words and devious purposes will bring confusion to our deliberations and calamities to the kingdom. Even if such people have managed to become virtuous citizens, they must not be permitted to take office and seek to extend their power.

Ninth, observe that the lords and the various office holders have had their stipends set according to the relative size of the country. The system is already fixed, and there must be no changes made in it. The ancient writings inform us that stipends should be allocated in accordance with the merits of those who receive them; positions should not be awarded for mere personal gain. If perchance someone quite without merit or someone possessing only some form of family connection should be awarded an office, not only will the people below him resent and object to it, but the person in question will not be able to enjoy his good fortune for long. Greatest vigilance must be observed in this regard. Furthermore, because we are surrounded by treacherous and powerful neighbors, even in peaceful times it will not do to become forgetful of the dangers. Honor those who serve in the military. Release them from corvée labor, and in the fall of each year, take care to recognize and promote those who have earned a special distinction.

Tenth, one who is responsible for a household or a state must always be alert for chance disasters. Read widely, therefore, in history and the classics, taking past events as lessons for the present. Though the Duke of Chou was a great sage, he instructed his nephew Sŏng Wang to read and heed *Without Idleness*. Prepare it in scroll form, affix it to the wall, and look at it always when entering or leaving the room. Reflect on it.

At the end of these ten injunctions, four Chinese characters were added saying, "keep these in your heart," so they would be treasured by the kings of future ages.

In May, the king's illness caused him so much discomfort, he brought a halt to his work of governance. Attended by ministers Yŏm Sang, Wang Kyu, and Pak Su-mun, the king finally spoke as follows.

As Emperor Mun of Han observed, there is nothing born that does not die. Death is the fundamental principle of heaven and earth; it is the nature of all things. So it is that the wise emperor thought of it, concerned that it become otherwise too overwhelmingly sad.

Some twenty days have now passed since I turned ill. Dying is a returning, so what is there to be anxious about? This is what I believe, just as the emperor did.

I want you to work with the crown prince on such long-standing matters of state as have not yet been resolved, then report to me.

On the next day, the king's illness turned severe. He was moved to Sindŏk Hall, and instructed the official Kim Ak to write down his final wishes. Once the draft was completed, the king could speak no more. All those in attendance broke into loud lamentations, at which the king asked, "What is that noise?" The attendants replied, "Our king has become like his subjects' own mother and father. Now it seems that today his majesty is suddenly about to leave his subjects. Our sorrow is overwhelming."

With a smile the king replied, "It has always been so, this fleeting life." Soon after speaking these words, the king died.

The king had been on the throne for twenty-six years. He was sixty-seven years old when he died.

Book 117: Biographies: Chŏng Mong-ju

With the dynasty founder T'aejo's (Yi Sŏng-gye) prestige steadily increasing, and the loyalty of the whole nation toward him growing as well, Chŏng Mong-ju became more aloof. He knew of Ta'ejo's intent to rule, in association with Cho Chun, Nam Un, Chŏng To-jŏn, and the others, and was therefore determined to seize whatever opportunity presented itself to get rid of T'aejo.

It happened that, as the crown prince Sŏk was returning from China, T'aejo had gone out to meet him at Hwangju. When he went hunting at Haeju, however, T'aejo suffered a fall from his horse and was incapacitated. Chŏng Mong-ju heard the news, and with a joyful expression on his face he sent the following instructions: "Yi Sŏng-gye has fallen from his horse and is in critical condition. We can accomplish our plan once we deal with his supporters, Cho Chun and the others." He immediately began to close in on Cho Chun, Chŏng To-jŏn, Nam Un, and some four or five others who had lent their support to T'aejo, intending to kill them as well as Yi T'aejo.

Meanwhile, T'aejo had returned as far as Pyŏngnando, where he planned to take lodging. His son T'aejong (Pang-wŏn) came to him and reported, "Chŏng Mong-ju is most certainly plotting to do us harm." When T'aejo still made no reply, T'aejong added, "We cannot remain here." T'aejo did not give his assent. Making another entreaty, T'aejong was finally able to assist his injured father to make his departure, and to complete the journey by palanquin back to the family compound that night. In his distress that the deed had not been accomplished, Chŏng Mong-ju went for several days without eating.

T'aejong asked his father, "What do you wish to do? The situation has become drastic." T'aejo replied, "Life and death are a matter of fate. We can only abide patiently." T'aejong consulted with his uncle's son-in-law Yi Che and several others, including military personnel. He said, "The Yi family renders loyal service to the throne. This is well known by all the people of this land. But now as a result of Chŏng Mong-ju's plot against us, we have come to have a bad reputation. Who will there be to redeem our family's honor in the future?" As they sought to deal with Chŏng Mong-ju, Pyŏn Chung-ryang, the son-in-law of T'aejo's elder brother, reported the details of their planning to Chŏng, who thereupon went to T'aejo's house to see for himself how things stood. T'aejo managed to treat him the same as always.

As soon as Chŏng left, T'aejong said, "If we lose this chance we are done for," and sent Cho Yŏng-gyu and five or six others after him. They attacked him on the road and killed him. Chŏng Mong-ju was fifty-six years old.

When T'aejong went in and reported this to T'aejo, he was greatly incensed at his son. In his injured state he struggled to rise, then angrily spoke to him, saying, "You have gone off on your own accord and killed the minister. Do you suppose the people of this land will actually think that I knew nothing about it? You were brought up to follow the dictates of loyalty and filiality, but now you have dared to commit this most unfilial act!"

T'aejong replied, "With Chŏng Mong-ju and his followers plotting against us, was I supposed to just sit and wait for disaster to befall us? My action was motivated by my filial concern. We must, in any event, call our loyal troops and have them make ready for any possible disturbance."

T'aejo reluctantly summoned Hwang Hŭi-sŏk and sent him to the king. He reported, "Chŏng Mong-ju was protecting criminals, and plotted against your loyal subjects. He has already received punishment. If you would summon Cho Chun, Nam Un, or others, they can present our vindication." After further close interrogation, the family and followers were sent into exile. Chŏng's head was taken and displayed in the street, along with a sign that read MADE EMPTY TALK, LED ASTRAY, PLOTTED AGAINST THE GOVERNMENT MINISTERS, AND CAUSED DISORDER TO THE STATE. As a further result of documents furnished by T'aejo's followers, all of Chŏng Mong-ju's property was confiscated.

Chŏng Mong-ju was a man of extraordinary talents, of bold vision, of principled loyalty and filiality. He studied diligently from earliest youth, conducted research in philosophy, and had many scholarly accomplishments. T'aejo always had the highest regard for his ability and would recommend him whenever he was on assignment in the various districts. He often put Chŏng's name forward for advancement to minister of state. His care and service for the state were outstanding. Chŏng Mong-ju managed major affairs and resolved a number of difficult problems. His manner and character were inflexible, while his responses to various matters were always appropriate to the situation. . . .

Under the present dynasty, (many) titles and honors were bestowed upon him. He had two sons, Chong-sŏng and Chong-pon.

SONG OF THE DRAGONS FLYING TO HEAVEN

Book 1

VERSE 1
Haedong's six dragons rise in flight,
their every deed heaven's gift,
the sign the same as the Ancient Worthies.

VERSE 2
The tree with deep roots does not tremble in winds;
its flowers are perfect, its fruit abundant.
Waters rising from deep sources do not vanish in drought;
forming a river they flow on to the sea.

VERSE 3
The King of Chou residing at Pin Valley
there began the works of empire.
Our ancestor residing in Kyŏnghŭng
there began the works of the kingdom.

VERSE 4
When he ventured among the barbarians
and the barbarians came to threaten,
he moved to Lofty Mountain,
and this was part of heaven's doing.

When he ventured among the Jurchen
and the Jurchen came to threaten,
he moved to Virtue Source,
and this was part of heaven's doing.

VERSE 5
The Late Worthy, the Duke of Chou,
told of a mud house by the banks of the rivers.
Those were the hardships
of founding an empire.

The mud hut on Chŏk Island
can still be seen today.
These were the hardships
of founding a kingdom.

VERSE 6
The virtue of Shang was waning;
one was about to take command of all beneath heaven.
The West River's banks were like a market,
filled with followers.

The cycle of Koryŏ was ending;
one was about to rule the country.
The shores of the East Sea were like a market,
filled with followers.

VERSE 7
Red bird holding a message
perched on the bedroom door,
portent of imperial joy
at the august son's revolution.

Snake carrying a magpie
draped it on the tree branch,
portent of future happiness
for the august grandson.

VERSE 8

Heaven chose the heir apparent;
older brother's intentions were fulfilled,
the august son
was born.

Heaven chose the crown prince;
the royal decree proclaimed,
the august grandson
was born.

VERSE 9

He took up the heavenly indictment;
the lords gathered from the four directions.
His saintly elevation was long established;
even the western barbarians gathered before him.

Proclaiming justice, he turned the army;
people gathered from miles around.
His sagaciousness was profound;
even the northern barbarians gathered before him.

Book 2

VERSE 10

One man set loose the evils of the world.
The people waited for the emperor.
With round baskets holding yellow silk
they looked for him along the wayside.

A madman committed boundless cruelties.
The people waited for the banner of justice.
With simple food in jugs and bowls
they looked for him along the wayside.

VERSE 11

When the petition of Wu and Ye was successful,
many came to him from the entire land,
but because his virtue was surpassing
he continued to serve the outcast.

When he stopped his army at Wihwa Island,
all put their trust and confidence in him,
but because his loyalty was surpassing
he enthroned a king restored.

VERSE 15

Leery of the region south of the Yangtze,
he dispatched an envoy,
but who could have blocked
the rise of the Seven Dynasties?

Leery of the region south of the Kongju River,
he admonished his descendants,
but were the prophecies of the Nine Transformations
merely a human's doing?

*There follow additional verses on the actions and attributes of the dynasty's
founders, until verse 25 finally reaches the granting of the royal robe to Yi
Sŏng-gye.*

VERSE 25

Such was his virtue,
the soldiers who started away
returned, and cloaked him
in the royal robe.

This was his loyalty,
that subjects who had died
and come back to life
cloaked him in the king's robe.

Additional verses describe the actions of the first rulers as they struggled to establish the new royal line. Verses 110–124 then present a remarkable series of admonitions to future monarchs. Two examples follow. Verse 125 is the final stanza.

VERSE 112
Pursuing the work of the king,
leading the army formations,
many were the days, one after another,
when he did not remove his armor.

When you stand draped
in the royal dragon robe
wearing a belt of precious jewels round your waist,
do not forget his example.

VERSE 116
Seeing the body on the road,
he gave up sleeping and eating,
refusing to look away from his tasks
even to see the autumn sky.

Heaven will abandon
those who care nothing
for the people in their afflictions,
so do not forget his example.

VERSE 125
One thousand years ago, in Hanyang,
the kingdom was established. The royal line may continue,
but only by worshipping heaven and serving the people
will the kingdom remain strong.
Oh King! Remember these things,
for if you go south on a hunting trip,
can you count on an ancestor to save it?

Sijo

The *sijo* is a three-line, vernacular verse form originally composed and sung to a fixed melody. *Sijo* continue to be written in the twentieth century, but as literary rather than musical works.

The usual *sijo* line comprises four rhythmic segments that correspond, in turn, to the grammatical divisions of the line. The segments generally vary between three and four syllables in length, but in line 3 the first segment is fixed at three syllables, the second at five or more, the third at four, and the last at three.

As the following selection shows, the subject matter ranges from philosophy to politics to love to playful silliness, from songs of nature to serious moral instruction, and sometimes loudly or quietly heroic moments. A common trope was the complaint at being forced to leave office and go into exile, but disguised as a sad song of lost affection, often in the voice or persona of a woman.

In the latter part of the Chosŏn dynasty the *sijo* form proved flexible both in subject matter and in such structural modifications as the *sasŏl sijo*, an expanded version. Chŏng Ch'ŏl's "Drinking Song," included here, is a well-known early example of *sasŏl sijo*.

The *kisaeng* whose *sijo* are included in the final group in this section were women entertainers, companions, courtesans. Very few direct records remain of their lives, and it is not unreasonable to suppose that some of them may even have been inventions, characters inhabiting the stories of ill-fated love that accompanied the *sijo* songs ascribed to them.

Sijo Songs

In one hand holding brambles,
      with the other grasping a big stick,
I tried to block the old road with brambles
      and chase white hairs off with my stick,
but white hairs knew my intent
      and came on by the furrowed road instead.

U T'ak (1263–1343)
      #2270 (see Notes)
The Korean original uses the phrase *chirŭm kil*, or *shortcut*, which is so
close to *churŭm*, *wrinkle*, that the pun is almost certainly intentional.

Once this body is dead and gone,
      you ask, what will it be?
On the highest peak of Pongnae Mountain,
      a towering, spreading pine.
When sky and earth are filled with white snow,
      alone and green, green, shall I be.

Sŏng Sam-mun (1418–1456)
      #1665

Since my mind turned foolish
      all I do is foolish.
Into these mountains wrapped in heavy clouds
      what love would ever come to find me?
Yet when the winds stir the falling leaves,
      I wonder who . . . Might it be . . . ?

Sŏ Kyŏng-dŏk (1489–1546)
      #713
Perhaps written in memory of his student, the *kisaeng* Hwang Chin-i.

The old ones haven't seen me
      and I haven't seen the old ones.
Though I have not seen the old ones,
      the path they walked lies before me.

Since the path they walked lies before me,
　　how could I not follow?

Yi Hwang (1501–1570)
　　#145

In the valley deep and green
　　are you sleeping, do you rest?
Where have you turned your lovely face
　　that bones alone lie buried here?
I raise the glass, but no one joins me.
　　I drink the sorrowful toast alone.

Im Che (1549–1587)
　　#867
Like Sŏ Kyŏng-dŏk's, above, said to have been written in memory of
Hwang Chin-i.

After the two have become man and wife,
　　then the children, brothers and sisters, are born.
Without the relation of man and wife
　　the Five Relations make no sense.
As far as the people are concerned,
　　the spousal relation is prime.

Pak Il-lo (1561–1642)
　　#948

Snow has come to the mountain village;
　　the stony road lies buried.
Do not open the brushwood gate.
　　Who would come looking for me?
But deep in the night, the bright sliver of moon:
　　You are my companion, I see!

Sin Hŭm (1566–1628)
　　#1061

Caught in the dusty winds of this world,
　　you cannot just shake off and go,

and the one dream of returning to streams and lakes
    is already long, long past.
Repay the royal favor,
    then start on the gladsome road back.

Kim Ch'ŏn-t'aek (18th c.)
    #2230

If black, they say white,
    and for white, they say black.
Black or white, not a one
    will say, "What difference does it make?"
Instead they block their ears, close their eyes,
    refusing to listen, refusing to see.

Kim Su-jang (1690–?)
    #122

Song of the Five Friends
Yun Sŏn-do (1587–1671)
    #s 423, 222, 157, 646, 332, 1816

Just how many friends have I?
    Water, stone, pine, and bamboo
And the moon rising on East Mountain:
    I am even more grateful for you.
Oh enough! What point could there be
    in claiming more friends than these?

The light in the clouds is lovely, true,
    but they will turn dark again.
The sound of the wind is fine and clear, true,
    but over and again simply ends.
Lovely, and unending:
    is not water the only such thing?

Why do flowers bloom
    only to fade and fall?
And the grasses growing green and tall,
    why so soon turn yellow?
What does not change at all?
    Stone alone, the only one.

The flowers bloom when it is warm,
    the petals fall in the chill.
How is it, Pine, even the blizzard
    does not seem to touch you?
It must be your roots run straight
    down to the Nine Springs below.

Not tree
    nor yet grass.
So straight, did someone plant you?
    Inside, such perfect emptiness.

Just so, and through all four seasons
    constant green: I am so fond of you.

Small, rising high
    to light up all the myriad things.
In the deep night, you alone
    are bright. Is there another?
And though you see, you say nothing.
    Are you my friend, I fondly hope?

Sijo songs by Chŏng Ch'ŏl (1536–1593)
  #s 811, 402, 1221, 93, 2281

In the water below, a shadow strikes;
    above, on the bridge, a monk is crossing.
O monk, stop there!
    Let me ask about where you are going.
With his staff, he points toward the white clouds
    and goes on, not turning to look back.

The tears she weeps for her dead husband
    flow down over her breasts;
The milk tastes salty,
    her child fusses and complains.
Poor thing! What is the purpose behind
    turning out to be a woman?

Snow has fallen in the pine woods,
    every branch blooming.
I shall break off one bough
    and send it to the place where my love stays.
If he just sees it once,
    what matter if it all melts away?

Rivers, lakes, buoyant
    the gull is.
Unexpectedly, spittle spat
    falls on the gull's back.
O gull, do not be angry.
    The ways of the world are filthy.

DRINKING SONG

Have a drink, won't you have another drink?
Pluck flowers to keep count, drink and drink and drink.

After this body dies, in a straw mat covered and roped to a
        pack frame
or carried along on a bier as thousands weep,
it will pass among willows, rushes, and oaks,
and when the sun shines yellow, the moon white,
rain drizzles down, or chill winds whirl the heavy snows,
who will say "Have a drink?"
And when some monkey sadly whistles on your grave,
what good will regrets be then?

Sijo Ascribed to *Kisaeng*

When did I deceive him?
    When was I untrue?
Yet halfway through this moonless night
    no sign that he will come at all.
Only the sound of leaves
    in an autumn wind—
      Why do I listen?

Hwang Chin-i (16th c.)
  #434

Alas, what have I done?
    Didn't I know how I would yearn?
Had I but bid him stay,
    how could he have gone? But stubborn
I sent him away,
    and now such longing learn!

Hwang Chin-i
  #1427

I hate it when you answer me
    as you would a child. Won't you change?
Were you beneath the skies alone,
    you might boast "I am all!"
But in all the heavens will provide
    is there no other love for me?

Munhyang (16th c.)
  #1492

A lover seen in dreams
    they say is faithless, so they say,
but driven by such distraction,
    how can I see, if not dreaming?

O love, show yourself
   and end this talk of dreams!

Maehwa (also attributed to Myŏngok)
   #255

I will take one branch of the willow
   and send it, my love, to you.
Plant it beneath your window
   and imagine when new leaves come
in the night rain
   it is I.

Hongnang (16th c.)
   #774

As the rain of pear blossoms fell and scattered
   I wept and held the love now gone.
In autumn winds and falling leaves
   I too may dream of flight,
though over the countless miles
   only these lonely dreams pass to and fro.

Kyerang (1513–1550)
   #1701

I will break the back
   of this long, midwinter night,
folding it double,
   cold beneath my spring quilt,
that I may draw out
   the night, should my love return.

Hwang Chin-i
   #672

Jade Green Stream, don't boast so proud
   of your easy passing through these blue hills.
Once you have reached the broad sea
   to return again will be hard.

While the Bright Moon fills these empty hills,
    why not pause? Then go on, if you will.

Hwang Chin-i
    #2056

Night descends on the mountain village;
    in the distance a watchdog barks.
I rise and open the brushwood gate
    to the moon in a cold sky.
But that dog! What does he mean with that din?
    To wake the moon on these hills?

Ch'ŏn'gŭm
    #1062

KASA

The *kasa* is the other major Korean vernacular verse form. It took the four-part line that also appears in the *sijo* to sometimes considerable lengths; travel *kasa*, records of journeys, could run on for hundreds of lines. Composition might be approached topically, by scenes, by stitching together brief lyric passages with longer narrative sections, or *durchkomponiert*, as it were, carrying a single story from beginning to end. The *kasa* form has been adapted to modern narrative poems and used by North Korean writers in socialist realist verse.

Chŏng Kŭg-in's "Song to Spring" is cited as the first example of the genre. "Song of Longing" by Chŏng Ch'ŏl is a famous example of a male poet using a female persona to express resentment at political misfortune. It is interesting to compare it with the *kasa* by Hŏ Nansŏrhŏn, a poem by a woman expressing resentment at her marital misfortune.

Pak Il-lo's "Song of a Humble Life" shows a remarkable control of colloquial narrative in the ox-borrowing scene, rather like one of Robert Frost's rustic tales. The opening lines of the poem refer to Pak's years of military service during the late sixteenth-century Japanese invasions of Korea.

Song to Spring
Chŏng Kŭg-in (1401–81)

You who are buried in the dust of this world,
    what do you think of my life?
Do I match, or do I not,
    the refinement of men of the past?
Though quite alone, the only man
    between earth and sky,
Would I not still know joy
    buried in these woods?
I build a small, thatched cottage
    close by the jade green stream,
and amid groves of pine and bamboo
    play host to the wind and moon.

Winter was gone a few days ago;
    as spring returns anew,
blossoms of peach and apricot
    bloom in the evening light,
while thick grasses and willows glow
    green in the misting rains.

Carved with a blade?
    Lined out with a brush?
Nature's creating spirit
    in all things calls out with joy.
The birds that sing in the thickets,
    overwhelmed completely by spring,
    are lovely, every voice.

Since nature and I are one,
    could our joys be separate?
As I walk out through the brushwood gate
    to rest in the arbor,
or wander along, reciting some verse,
    can mountain days be lonely?

The true meaning of leisure, to others
    unknown, is mine alone.

Listen to me, neighbors! Let us go
    view the hills and streams.
Let us walk through the fields today
    and bathe in the stream tomorrow;
in the morning gather greens on the mountain,
then fish in the stream at evening.
Let us take the fresh-brewed wine,
    strain it through a hat,
and drink, plucking flowers
    from a branch to keep count.

Gentle breezes swiftly blowing
    cross the green waters;
the noble fragrance sinks in the cups,
    and petals fall over our clothes.
Tell me when the flagon is empty;
    I will send the boy
    to the tavern for wine.

The old man grasps his stick;
    the boy lifts the wine to his shoulder.
Quietly reciting, I settle down
    alone by the side of the stream.
In the clean, bright sand I scour
    the cup, fill, and raise it.
Looking down on the clear waters
    I see peach blossoms.
Fabled Murŭng must be near.
    These domains must be the place.

Through pines on a narrow path,
    clasping azaleas in my arms,
I reach the very topmost heights
    and gaze down from the clouds.

Thousands of hamlets, myriad villages
    spread out below, everywhere.
Fog and mist and the sun's brightness
    seem to weave a brocade
as fields that lay dark a few days ago
    are flooded with colors of spring.

Renown escapes me,
    wealth and rank spurn me,
but the clear moon and bright sun—
    what other friends would I have?
With gourd, basket, and wretched shelter,
    my thoughts are free of confusion.
Tell me then, for a hundred years' pleasure,
    what could surpass just this?

Song of Longing
Chŏng Ch'ŏl (1536–93)

At the time I was born
    I was born to follow my lord.
Our lives were destined to be joined,
    as even the heavens must have known.

When I was young
    my lord loved me.
There was nothing to compare
    with this heart and love.
All that I longed for in this life
    was to live with him.

Now that I am older,
    for what reason have I been put aside?
A few days ago, serving my lord
    I entered the Moon Palace.
How does it happen since then
    that I have descended to this lower world?
Three years it has been
    since my hair, once combed, became tangled.
I have powders and rouge,
    but for whom would I make myself lovely?
The cares that are knotted in my heart
    pile up, layer upon layer.
It is sighs that build up,
    tears that tumble down.
Life has an end;
    cares are endless.

Indifferent time
    is like the flowing of waters.
The seasons, hot and cold, seem to know
    time and return as they go.

Hearing, seeing,
>there are many things to sense.

Briefly the east wind blows
>and melts away the fallen snow.
Two or three branches have bloomed
>on the plum tree outside the window:
a bold brightness,
>a fragrance deep and mysterious.
At dusk the moon
>shines by the bedside
as if sensing him, rejoicing
>—Is it my lord; could it be?
I wonder, if I broke off that blossom
>and sent it to the place where my lord stays,
what would he think
>as he looked at it?

Blossoms fall, new leaves appear,
>and shade covers.
Silk curtains are lonely;
>embroidered curtains are opened.
I close the lotus screen
>and open the peacock screen . . .
How can a day be so tedious,
>so full of cares?
I spread open the mandarin duck quilt,
>take out the five-colored thread,
measure it with a golden ruler
>and make a cloak for my lord
with skill,
>with taste.

Gazing toward the place where my lord stays
>I think of sending to him
these clothes in a jade white chest
>on a pack frame of coral,

but he is so far, so far,
    like a mountain, or a cloud.
Who is there to seek him out
    over the road of ten thousand *li*?
When it reached him and was opened,
    would he be pleased?

At night a frost falls;
    the wild goose passes over with a cry.
Alone, I climb the tower
    and open the jade curtain.
Above East Mountain the moon has risen
    and far to the north a star appears.
Is it my lord? Happy,
    tears come unbidden.
Let me extract this brightness
    and send it to the Phoenix Tower:
fix it to the tower
    and illuminate all directions,
that even the deepest mountains and valleys
    may be as bright as day.

Heaven and earth are blockaded
    under a white monochrome.
Men, even birds on the wing
    have disappeared.
With the cold so intense
    here, far to the south,
in the lofty Phoenix Tower
    how much colder it must be!
Would that the sunny spring could be sent
    to warm the place where my lord stays,
or that the sunlight bathing the thatched eaves
    might be sent to the Phoenix Tower.

I tuck my red skirt up,
    roll my blue sleeves halfway,

and as the day declines, by high, thin bamboos
　　I lean on a staff, lost in thought.
The brief sun sinks swiftly;
　　　the long night settles aloft.

I set the inlaid lute
　　by the side of the blue lamp
and rest, hoping
　　to see my lord, even in a dream.
Cold, cold is the quilt!
　　O, when will night become day?

Twelve times each day,
　　thirty days each month,
I try, even for a moment, not to think,
　　that I may forget these cares,
but they are knotted within my heart,
　　they have pierced through my bones.
Even though ten doctors like P'ien Ch'üeh came,
　　what could they do with this illness?
Alas, my illness
　　is because of my lord.

I would rather die and become
　　a swallowtail butterfly.
I would light upon each flowering branch
　　one after another, as I went,
till I settled, with perfumed wings
　　upon the garments of my lord.
O, my lord, though you forget my existence,
　　I shall attend you.

Song of a Humble Life
Pak Il-lo (1561–1643)

Careless and foolish—
    no one more so than I.
Good fortune or bad,
    leaving all to heaven,
in a wretched, hidden-away place
    I build a thatched hut.

For kindling, straw soaked
    with wind and rain, morning to night.
My portions of gruel and rice
    taste mostly of smoke.
Lukewarm rice water is all I have
    to deceive my empty belly.

Even in a life like this
    a man's purpose does not change.
At peace in privation, remaining steadfast:
    I cherish this thought.
I live in accord with propriety,
    but day after day goes awry.

Should there be scarcity in autumn
    let the spring bring plenty;
should the purse be empty
    let the bottle be full.

I am not alone
    in this miserable existence.
Though starving and cold, and clad in rags,
    I shall not omit fidelity.

Forgetting myself in devotion to duty,
    determined, though confronting death,

for five years of war
    unafraid to die
I trod upon corpses, forded rivers of blood,
    and suffered through numberless battles.

Free again,
    I sought this house.
The long-bearded servant had forgotten
    the distinction between master and man;
I doubt that he will inform me
    of the arrival of spring.

I may have to ask some serf
    when they plough the fields,
for I know I must plough
    and plant the fields alone.
This old man out weeding the fields
    is not mean,
but however much I want to plough
    I need the ox.

A long dry spell;
    the change in seasons is late.
The brief rain
    on the high, west field
runs off
    like water from a road.
On a moonless night I push my steps
    to the house where I had a kind of promise
    for the loan of an ox.

I stand alone
    outside the tight-shut gate,
cough loudly,
    and after a while hear
    "Well, who is out there?"

"Shameless I."

"What brings you out
    at this hour of the night?"

"I am in need like this
    every year, I know,
but there is no ox at my poor house,
    only many debts, so I have come."

"I know I said I would loan it
    for nothing, or a little,
but last night the fellow
    from the house across the way
cooked up a red-throated pheasant
    all dripping with juices,
and had me drinking fresh spring wine
    till I was tipsy.
Thinking I simply had to repay
    such generosity
I made him the promise
    of the loan of my ox tomorrow.
I would be ashamed to break a promise.
    What can I say?"

"Well, if that is so
    there is nothing to be done."

With shabby hat drooping, in worn-down sandals,
    dispiritedly I trace my way home.
At my crestfallen appearance
    the dog starts barking.

Entering my snail shell room,
    sleepless I stand
leaning by the north window,
    waiting for dawn.

The heartless cuckoo
    echoes my rancor.
In distress I watch
    the fields until dawn.
The pleasant farmer songs
    sound spiritless.
Baffled sighs have no end.

With that precious plough
    and ploughshare hanging on the wall,
even the old, thorn-choked field
    could be handily turned,
but without a thing to use
    I am at a loss.

The ploughing season passes;
    everything is swept away.

It is long since I dreamed
    of the rivers and lakes,
for I have lived till now
    worried about mouth and belly.
I see on the banks of the Ch'i
    the bamboos grow thick.

O illustrious ones,
    lend me a fishing pole.

Where the flowering reeds are deep
    I befriend the bright moon, clear breeze,
and amid the ownerless moon and winds, mountains, and rivers
    I shall grow older and older.

Indifferent gull,
    would you summon, or send me away?
One who would not be quarrelsome—
    you must be that one.

There may be some purpose
 for this old frame.
I have let one or two
 of the fields go fallow,
so if there is anything to eat, it is gruel,
 and if nothing, I starve.
I feel no envy
 for another's goods, another's house.
Though I despise my poverty,
 can I raise a hand and send it away?
If I covet another's wealth and honor,
 can I summon them with a gesture?
There is nothing that happens in this life
 that is not by fate.

To be free of resentment even in poverty
 is difficult, it is told,
but though my life goes on like this
 there is nothing sad about it.
A dipper of water, a measure of rice;
 these are sufficient.
Warm clothes and a full belly
 are not the purpose of life.

For loyalty and filiality to flourish
 in this time of peace,
who could find fault with
 concord among relations, trust among friends?
As for the rest, whatever remains to be done
 let it happen just as it will.

Married Sorrow
Hŏ Nansŏrhŏn (1563–1589)

Just yesterday, it seemed, I was young.
　　How did it happen? Am I suddenly old?
The joys of youth! Even
　　to think of recalling them is useless.
I am so old. To try
　　just to speak the words makes my throat grow tight.
My mother and father together
　　took such pains to raise me,
thinking at least to find a good man
　　if not some grand official for my spouse.
Destined to be married,
　　through the go-between's advising
I met the merry man of the capital.
　　It all seems now like a dream.
I was oh, so very careful then,
　　as if stepping on thin ice.

When at last I turned sixteen
　　with that disposition,
my face, its expression,
　　I vowed one hundred years together,
but time passes so quickly,
　　jealousies multiply.
Spring wind, autumn moon pass
　　back and forth like a shuttle through the cloth.
Where did that sweet face go,
　　that this hateful expression now possesses it?
Looking at this face, I wonder
　　who ever could love me.
Shame rises through me,
　　but who is there to accuse?

Nightly pleasures taken by threes and fives,
    and a new man seemed to appear.
When flowers bloomed as the day was growing dark,
    he went off wandering
on a white horse with his golden whip.
    Where, where is he lingering?
I do not know whether he is near or far.
    If only there were some word!
How can I not fear
    that this time the bond is broken?

To descend into longing
    for not seeing his face!
Each day, each day is long;
    thirty days become endless tedium.
The plum I planted outside the window
    has bloomed and faded many times over.
Each winter night, night after night is cold,
    while the thick snows fall and tangle.
Summer, day after day is long;
    the heavy rains fall for no reason.
Flowers and willows stirring,
    the spring days are a welcome season,
but though the scene is all that it should be
    my heart knows no ease.

Autumn enters the room,
    and a cricket sadly cries.
Useless thoughts attend
    my long sighs and falling tears.
However wretched this life of mine,
    to die would be hard.
Think, rather, whether to try
    this, or try that;
turn the lamp,
    set the zither in place,

and play the Lotus Suite melody,
    though all distracted by grief.

It sounds like the bamboo leaves
    in the night rain by the rivers;
or like the crane that cries "Live a thousand years"
    from the stone set by the lonely tomb.

Though I lift my voice
    as my fingers ply the strings,
with the lotus curtain drawn closed,
    how could the sound reach his ear?
As my insides melt with pain
    that breaks apart, piece by piece,
let me at last fall asleep,
    let me at least have a dream.

Leaves that fall in the wind,
    creatures crying in the bushes,
am I then your enemy,
    that you deny me even my sleep?
The heavenly herdsman and the weaver maid,
    though the Milky Way bars their crossing,
once a year, the seventh of the seventh month,
    have their moment, do they not?
Since my love has gone,
    light as water ferried away,
there is not a word, none at all,
    whether he might return or go on, farther away.

Pressing against the railing,
    I look off in his direction.
Dew gathers on the leaves,
    evening clouds pass over,
while deep in the bamboo groves
    the cries of the birds grow sadder.

They say that life is full
of unhappy loves. So they say.
But could a youthful springtime
be more unhappy than mine?
Thoughts of him make me suffer so,
I know not whether I live or die.

HANMUN: POEMS AND PROSE IN CHINESE

Perhaps the second most noteworthy feature of Korean literature written in literary Chinese is that it does not constitute a monolithic structure. The corpus of works in Chinese is various in form, philosophical underpinnings, and views on language, diction, the past, the proper subject, the purpose of the whole enterprise of writing. Yi Kyu-bo (1168–1241), for example, one of the most compelling figures in Korean letters, composed poems in literary Chinese that reflected the difficult life of farming during the extended period when the court was living in luxury on Kanghwa Island, safe from the depredations of the invading Mongol armies. His poems can certainly be read as protests against the conditions of the time, but that would in turn make them criticisms of the ruling Ch'oe family, his official sponsors. Yi's long poem in praise of Chumong, King Tongmyŏng of Koguryŏ, a paean to local, Korean mythical tales and indigenous cultural accomplishments, can be read against the grain of such Chinese-model historical works as Kim Pu-sik's *History of the Three Kingdoms, Samguk sagi* (1145). In other words, the fact that it was written in Chinese does not determine a text's ideological or cultural outlook. To take a later example, Pak Chi-wŏn (1737–1805) wrote all of his works in Chinese, but focused on the literary enterprise as a means of pursuing inquiry rather than simply as a way to express an accepted, received truth in a refined manner. Thus he introduced a revolutionary view of literature as discovery. The literary historian Cho Tong-il also notes of Pak's work that while it was meant as a form of social criticism, it was not deployed as a means for personal advancement.[1]

Of course the first thing to notice about Chinese-language materials is the vast depth and breadth of the corpus. In just one exemplary anthology, the *Collection of Eastern Writing, Tongmun sŏn,* edited by Sŏ Kŏ-jŏng and distributed in 1478, more than 4,000 works by some 400 writers were included. A supplement, *Sok tongmun sŏn,* was edited and released in 1518 in an additional 21 volumes. To take a contemporary example, Hŏ Kyŏng-jin's series of anthologies of Korean *hansi,* poems in Chinese, translated into modern Korean had already reached volume 40, a gathering of 150 poems by Chosŏn-dynasty Buddhist monks, in 1997. Yet even the vast body of Chinese-language works by Korean writers has been the subject of dispute as to whether or not it constitutes a legitimate part of the Korean literary canon. Following the end of the Japanese colonial occupation, there was a tendency in Korean scholarly circles to attempt to redefine the Korean cultural heritage in indigenous terms, which meant, among other things, that Chinese-language literary works were denigrated or dismissed entirely. North Korea dropped Chinese characters from contemporary language use, yet also pursued a number of projects to translate the Chinese-language literary and historical heritage into modern Korean. At present, the answer to the question about the Korean-ness of Chinese-language literary and other works has been allowed to resolve itself in the affirmative.

Simply to give a sense of the field, I have chosen a small number of *hanmun* texts. Ch'oe Ch'i-wŏn (ninth century) lived at the very end of the Silla period, and many of his poems reflect his decision to withdraw from public office. Kim Pu-sik (1075–1171), the well-known Koryŏ military leader, statesman, and literatus, was chosen to produce the *History of the Three Kingdoms, Samguk sagi.* His poem about Kwallan Temple expresses what seems a self-deprecatory attitude, but at the same time it is written from the top, with the poet looking down, literally and figuratively, on a world that seems no more three-dimensional than a painting. Kim was also in every sense of the term a nasty piece of political work, and did away with his political enemies and literary rivals—most notably, Chŏng Chi-sang—with relish. Yi Kyu-bo (1168–1241) seems to be located at ground level. His poems about the world at large are closely observed rather than distant and express an empathetic understanding of others, while his poems about himself and his family are full of rueful humor.

Im Che was famous for his Coleridge-like withdrawal from the world of the capital and his energetic touring of the countryside. The two *hansi* selections have something of the taste of set pieces, especially his poem in the voice of a woman, while his *sijo* poem remembering the *kisaeng* Hwang Chin-i could record an actual visit to the site of her tomb. It is interesting, though, to compare his or any other male writer's works—another example would be Chŏng Ch'ŏl's "Longing for the Beautiful One"—with those of Hŏ Nansŏrhŏn (1563–1589). The immensely talented and unfortunate sister of Hŏ Kyun (1569–1618), she was the mother of two children who died in infancy and the wife, evidently, of someone who made up for his comparative intellectual deficiencies by constant womanizing. Her poems are not noted for breaking new ground in a technical sense but were accorded a great deal of respect at the time they were gathered and published by her younger brother Hŏ Kyun; in the years since they have continued to elicit admiration for their clarity and great sympathy for the depths of sorrow they express.

The assortment of a few *hansi* by other women that closes this section shows, among other things, the casual expressive possibilities of the Chinese poetic medium, and suggests that such expression was not entirely restricted to the male population, though it does seem a rather upper-class phenomenon. Finally, it is interesting to compare the *hansi* by Lady Chŏng (1598–1680), "Saints," with the *sijo* verse by the Confucian scholar Yi Hwang (1501–1570), "The old ones haven't seen me . . ." to observe a woman's Chinese-language and a man's Korean vernacular expressions on a common literary theme.

Pak Chi-wŏn's "The Story of Master Hŏ," "*Hŏsaeng chŏn*," is included in his account of a journey to Beijing, the *Yŏrha ilgi*, of 1780. It contains a range of materials, some of which, including "Master Hŏ," are introduced as records of some other person's tale—in this case, a storyteller named Yun. This may have been a ploy to avoid direct rebuke for the story's satire. Given the general *sirhak* program of "censure of those who held political power and a consequent intent to bring about changes in the political and social order,"[2] the satirical critique of contemporary Korean society and its timid, ineffectual leadership is somewhat predictable. The proposition at the end of the story, though—that Korea could recover its national dignity and bring down the Manchu (Ch'ing) rulers of China by starting a covert political movement through the posting of talented young men to China in the guise of merchants—is startling.

The record of the reception or circulation of such materials as Pak

Chi-wǒn's story affords an intriguing series of glimpses into the history of modern as well as pre-modern Korean literary and political-ideological culture. During the Japanese colonial occupation of Korea, the novelist Yi Kwang-su (1879–1951?) published a serial translation of the story in the newspaper *Tonga Ilbo* (1923–1924). The translation grafted a modern message about Korean progressivism, exemplified in Master Hǒ's entrepreneurial spirit and action, to what under the apparent radical proposal to do away with the existing, Manchu order is an extremely conservative message: that Korea can and should return to its proper relationship with the true rulers of China, the Ming, not the Ch'ing usurpers. Three decades later in North Korea, the story was read as a critique of the class structure of traditional Korean society: the "Biographical Note" in the 1954 collection of Pak Chi-wǒn's works translated by Ch'oe Ik Han and Hong Ki Mun observes Pak's upper-class apostasy, and how "through the mouth" of the character of Master Hǒ, Pak criticized the *yangban* class from which he had come, portraying a society purged of class divisions by a popular uprising of the peasant farmers.[3] A translation of the complete *Yǒrha ilgi* by Yi Ka-wǒn, published in Seoul in 1968, gives the tale the colloquial flavor of the scene of the late-night visit in Pak Il-lo's "Song of a Humble Life."

Hansi by Yi Kyu-bo and Others

TO THE MASTER OF KŬMCH'ŎN TEMPLE

In white clouds by the stream's edge you built this shrine.
Thirty years now since you came here, and still you stay.
Smiling, by the gate you show the way suddenly before me.
Descending the mountain, it ravels into a thousand different
    paths.

Ch'oe Ch'i-wŏn (9th c.)

AUTUMN NIGHT RAIN

Autumn wind; reciting only bitter poems.
Down the roads of the world, few would fathom the sound.
Outside the window, third hour past midnight and raining.
By the lamp, thoughts reach out ten thousand *li*.

Ch'oe Ch'i-wŏn

AT KWALLAN TEMPLE

Six months, the heat of human affairs intense.
One whole day at the river terrace, and the clear wind is
    sufficient.
The mountains' shapes, the waters' colors have no past, no
    present.
Worldly events and people's hearts have their likeness and
    difference.
The boat sculls all alone into the center of the mirror;
without its mate, the partridge flies through the center of the
    picture.
The more endured, the more it seems life is like the horse's bit:
it won't ease for the infirmities of one bald old man.

Kim Pu-sik (1075–1171)

A WIFE'S RESENTMENT

Fifteen-year-old girl from Wŏlgye,
shy of others, wordless has slipped away.

Inside the inner gate,
someone weeps at the pear blossom moon.

Im Che (1549–1587)

MOUNTAIN TEMPLE

Half night, in the forest; the monk is sleeping.
Heavy clouds soak the clothes and the grass.
On the crag, a door opens: the late evening sun.
Roosting birds startle into flight.

Im Che

POEMS BY YI KYU-BO (1168–1241)
WHITE HERONS AND SMARTWEED

Fish and shrimp, lots, in the shallows below.
White heron splits the waves, advancing.
Seeing a person, startled, it rises
and flies off, lighting on the hilltop covered with smartweed.
Neck bending, it waits for the person to pass by,
its feathers getting wetter in the drizzle.
The man says, "Look at it standing there, not a thought in its
        head
about all those fish in the waves."

TO SAMBAEK, MY SON, DRINKING YOUNG

1.

You know already how to tip the wine jar;
before many years pass you may bust a gut, so stop.
Don't follow your father's example, always tipsy.
All your life, people will be calling you a crazy fellow.

2.

The ruination of my life, that's what wine has been,
so I wonder why even now you seem to like it.
I wish I had not gone and named you *Sambaek*,
for you may indeed wind up drinking *three hundred* cups a day.

STRAW FOR THE BURNING

Making poems since I was young,
just grabbed a brush and couldn't stop.
I was so proud of my lovely jewels,
and who was bold enough to point out their flaws?
Now at a later day I search through them again,
and in poem after poem, there is not a decent line.
I can't filthy up my writing box with the stuff,
so I shove it all in the kitchen stove and burn it.
Even what I wrote last year, when I looked
I just got rid of it too, like the other trash.
The eminence of poets of old lay in this:
they did not write a thing till they passed fifty.

TWO VERSES ON THE MOON IN A WELL

1.

From deep in the clear well water by the mossy green rock,
the newly risen moon shines straight back.
In the water bottle I filled, the half moon sparkles.
I carry back only one half of the moon round as a mirror.

2.

Mountain monk wanted it, the bright moonlight,
so he drew enough water to fill the whole jar.
Returned to the temple; only then did he find,
when water spills from the jar, the moon spills too.

IMPROMPTU

Wineless, I am verseless;
verseless, I want no wine.
I delight in both wine and verse;
they go so well together, they cannot be apart.
Where my hand inclines, I may have written some verse,
and as my mouth inclines, I may have drunk a bit of wine.
How did it happen, that this tidy old man
came to the practices of wine and verse together?
I never managed to drink too much wine,

for the verses do not add up to so many.
When I am facing a cup, my joy just leaps up.
It is hard to know how to change that frame of mind.
As my illness grows worse I realize
the only cure for my affliction will be to die.
It is all most distressing, and not only to me;
because of it, others are scolding me constantly.

EVENING VIEW
Li Po and Tu Fu squawked and it's done,
heaven and earth left in desolation.
Only the mountains and rivers quite at peace
as a crescent moon hangs in the sky's vast space.

Hansi by Hŏ Nansŏrhŏn (1563–1589)

AT MY SON'S GRAVE

One year ago I lost my beloved daughter;
this year I lost my beloved son.
How sad, how sad this expanse of tombs,
where two graves line up facing each other.
In the poplar branches the wind desolately cries;
in the pine grove, spirit fires gleam.
Scattering the paper money I call your soul;
I pour the cup of wine on your grave.
May your lonely souls, brother and sister,
play joyfully each night as before you were born.
A baby is growing inside, I know, but how
will I know if I can raise the child, as things go?
Lost in grief I repeat this lament;
with tears of blood, I choke down each bitter note.

CONTEMPLATION

Delicate petals of the orchid in the window,
so piercing, their fragrance.
Let the autumn wind just pass through them,
they begin to wilt at the cold touch of frost.
Their shape begins to change, to fall,
but their clear fragrance does not die.
Seeing their form, my heart aches,
my tears fall, my sleeves are wet.

SENDING OFF

Yellow gold, beautifully wrought,
the half-moon pendant was a gift
from my in-laws when I came in marriage.
I hung it on my red silk gown.
I give it to you, my love, as you start off today,
hoping you will look at it as a token of my love.
It will not be so awful if you leave it on the way,
just do not hand it over as a gift to some new love.

TO MY ELDER BROTHER

By the dark window a candle flame flickers low;
the lights of the fireflies climb up over the roof.
The deep, dark night turns colder;
whispering, the leaves are falling and scattering.
Mountain and stream blocking the way, not much news gets
through.
I cannot ease my concerns as I am thinking of you.
How I miss you, far from where you stay at the Blue Lotus
Palace!
Deep in these vacant hills, only the moon shines through the
vines.

THE YOUNG SEAMSTRESS

How can this worn face appeal?
Working at embroidery, then returning to work at the weaving
from behind a gate where there is little or nothing and long
without heat.
The matchmaker won't let anyone know of one so meek.

Cold, starving, but the expression does not show it;
all day by the window weaving the hempen cloth.
Only father thinks it pitiful, but others in the place,
how will they ever know of me?

All night without rest weaving the hempen cloth,
the loom going *clack-clack, clack-clack,* a chilly sound.
Weave one roll on the loom, and wonder
for whose house, whose daughter will it be a dowry?

Scissors in hand, cut the cloth in pieces;
and though the night is cold, all ten fingers are straight.
I make clothes for others going to be married,
while year after year, it is I who must sleep alone.

Hansi by Lady Chŏng and Other Women

SAINTS

Not born in the time of the saints,
cannot see their faces.
But the words of the saints can be heard,
their hearts can be seen as well.

Lady Chŏng, of the Chang Family (1598–1680)

CRYING RAIN

Outside the window the rain weeps down;
all of nature is a sound of weeping.
When I hear nature's sound,
my heart also finds its nature.

Lady Chŏng

THE JOYS OF COUNTRY LIFE

The servant girl went to market this morning.
She came back with firewood, as much as she could carry.
Plant mulberry trees to the south and west,
and I can raise silkworms for thread.

Madam Sin, known as Pu Yong Tang (1732–?)

ON A LINE FROM LI PO

A sound there is in the trees, a cold, confusing
wind in the forest as birds cry, returning in evening light.
The night is clear. Stand alone and look toward home:
frost covers the fields, moonlight covers the mountains.

Lady Sŏ, Yŏng Su-hap (1753–?)

The Story of Master Hŏ
Yŏnam, Pak Chi-wŏn (1737–1805)

Master Hŏ lived in Mŏkchŏk. Just below South Mountain, right where an old apricot tree grows by the well, directly across is a small twig gate, always open. Inside the gate was a thatched-roof cottage. The roof was old and worn out, not enough to keep out the wind and rain.

The master of the house, known simply as Master Hŏ, loved to read books. His wife did piecework sewing, and just barely made ends meet. One day, when her stomach felt completely empty, she wailed, "You haven't even tried to take the state examination. All you do is read read read. What is the point of it? Don't you even feel hungry?"

Hŏ laughed and, setting his book aside, replied, "Be patient just a little longer. I haven't finished reading everything yet."

"No! You have to do something! Things cannot go on like this. Go and do some work, somewhere. Keep us from starving, will you?"

"But what do I know about working? The only thing I know is what I have learned from books."

"Well, what about selling things?"

"That's impossible. I don't have the money to get started."

His wife grew angrier and angrier. She yelled at him, "Listen! Day and night, all you do is read! Is this all you have learned? You can't work, you can't sell! Why don't you go and try being a thief?"

With his wife nagging constantly, there wasn't a thing he could do. Master Hŏ closed his book, stood up, and saying, "What a waste! I wanted to study for ten years, and here I have only managed seven," he walked out the door.

Hŏ didn't know a soul in the place, so he went to the market street in the capital and asked, "Who is the richest man around here?" The market people replied, "Pyŏn the rich man. He's the richest there is."

As soon as he heard this, Master Hŏ set off to find the rich man's house. Once there, with no more than a quick knock at the door by way of introduction, he walked in and said, "Look here. I am poor, but there is something I want to try. Loan me ten thousand *ryang*."

Pyŏn heard just that much and replied, "Good. I'll do it," and without a moment's hesitation, handed over the money on the spot.

Carrying the ten thousand, Hŏ turned and went out, without a word of thanks.

Staying at Pyŏn's house there were, at the time, a large number of retainers, stewards, laborers, attendants, and general hangers-on. They all thought that Master Hŏ was nothing more than a beggar. His appearance was shabby. His belt was worn out, the heels of his shoes had collapsed, instead of a proper horsehair hat on his head he had perched a cap, his coat was full of holes, and because of the cold, his nose was runny. As soon as this beggar had gone out the gate, the hangers-on, eyes wide in disbelief, asked, "Do you know that fellow?"

Pyŏn replied, "I don't know who he is."

"A person you never saw before, never heard of, a complete stranger, it seems? You gave him ten thousand *ryang*, just like that? That is a huge sum! And you didn't even ask him his name?"

Pyŏn answered, "This is not a matter that the likes of you would easily understand. Usually when people ask for money, first of all they talk and talk about their scheme, and they try very hard to look sincere. But it never fails: they can't keep the uncertainty out of their faces, and their words sound forced and hollow. But this fellow just now: his clothes and shoes were in tatters, but his words were clear and direct. His eyes were steady; there was no sign of nervousness in his face. He is someone who disdains material possessions, but he does possess a strong inner drive. It is very likely that his plan will succeed, so I decided to give him the chance. I don't know about his name if I had decided against him, but once I had made up my mind, what point would there have been in asking it?"

After getting the ten thousand *ryang* from Pyŏn the rich man, instead of returning to his home, Master Hŏ set off on the road to the south. He went as far as the marketplace in Ansŏng, down between Kyŏnggi and Ch'ungch'ŏng provinces, where the three major roads to the south all came together. He settled in and started doing business.

Master Hŏ bought chestnuts, dates, persimmons, pears, and tangerines, paying twice the normal price for them. He bought the fruit in bulk, all of it, so that no one anywhere could find any. It became impossible to prepare feasts and ceremonies.

Before long, as the demand grew even more intense and no one could tell where the price might go, the merchants who had been happy to sell their goods for double came flocking to Master Hŏ, glad to give him ten times the normal amount to buy them back.

Suddenly rich, Master Hŏ let out a sigh and said, "So, all it takes is ten thousand *ryang* to get to the bottom of our country's resources."

With the money he had made, Master Hŏ turned to necessities like knives and hoes, or hemp cloth, silk, and cotton. He bought them up, then went to Cheju Island and bought up all the horse tail and mane hair. He said to himself, "In a year, no one in the whole country will be able to cover his head." Indeed, before long, the prices had all gone up ten times.

One day Master Hŏ was visiting the coast when he saw an old man, a boatman. He asked him, "Are there any empty islands out there where people could go and live?"

The old man replied, "There are. Once I was caught in a storm. I was driven east for four days and nights. I landed on an empty island; it seemed to lie between Samun and Nagasaki. I found fruit trees and bushes there, deer large and small, in herds, and even the fish weren't afraid when they saw a human."

Master Hŏ was delighted at the old boatman's reply. The fellow seemed most sincere. He said to the old man, "If you will take me to the island, I will share my fortune with you. What do you say?"

The old fellow quickly agreed. So the two of them caught a favoring wind and headed southeast. When they reached the island and had landed, Master Hŏ climbed a hill and looked around in all four directions. He seemed greatly disappointed. "What can be done in such a small place? At least the earth is fertile and the streams are fresh, so I suppose I can try living here like a rich man."

The old boatman was puzzled by Hŏ's reference to living like a rich man. "On such a deserted isle, with not another living soul here, who would you be living with then?"

Hŏ replied at once, "Virtue will bring people. That's not the problem. What worries me is that I lack virtue."

At this time in the Pyŏnsan region of Chŏlla Province, there were a thousand or so people known as the Band of Thieves holding out. The local militia had been sent out to capture them but had failed. Even so, it had become impossible for the robber band to go out and conduct their operations. They were, in fact, starving and in great distress. Master Hŏ got wind of the situation and found his way to their camp by himself. Finding the leader of the robbers, Hŏ started to talk with him.

"If the thousand of you somehow got hold of a thousand *ryang*, how much would that be for each one?"

"Why, one *ryang* each."

"Do any of you have wives?"

"No. No wives."

"Farm fields? How about fields?"

"Listen here! If we had wives and fields, do you think we would still be wanting to live the horrible lives we do, as bandits?"

At their leader's retort, several of his followers burst into laughter.

"Well, if you really mean that, then would it not be better for you to get married, build houses, do the farming, and stop being bandits? Your lives would be happy, you wouldn't be worried about going out and getting caught, and you would have food and clothing in plenty. Wouldn't that be wonderful?"

"Oh, it would be! But how can we? We don't have the money!"

Master Hŏ laughed at this. "So how is it that thieves like you are still worried about not having money? I have a plan. Go to the shore tomorrow and look for the boats flying the red flags. They will all be loaded with money. Take as much as you want."

With this promise, Master Hŏ went off. The bandits exclaimed after he had gone, "What is all that? What is he talking about?" and laughed at him for being a complete madman. Even so, the arrangement had been made with such certainty that on the following day they all went to the shore together, and there they discovered that the strange traveler had brought a number of ships, all with red flags flying. Each one was loaded with thirty thousand *ryang*. They were astounded. They lined up in front of him and bowed down until their noses touched the ground.

"Your wish is our command," they chorused.

Hŏ replied, "You can't carry more than a hundred *ryang* each. How could you think you could ever steal enough? Even if you wanted to go back to normal lives, with the government calling you bandits, where could you go? Listen. I will wait for you. Each one of you, take a hundred *ryang*. Find yourself a wife and an ox, then come back. That is all."

"Yes! We shall obey," they replied, and scattered in all directions.

Hŏ then assembled a year's provisions for two thousand people. He waited. Of the Band of Thieves, every one of them without exception came back as agreed. So he gathered them into the boats, entering them into his ledger books by their thumbprints. And since Master Hŏ had taken away the Band of Thieves in his boats, for a time the region knew an interval of freedom from banditry.

As soon as they had landed, Hŏ's followers began to cut down trees and build houses, and to construct bamboo fences. The soil was so fertile, everything they planted grew tall. So luxuriant was it, not a field lay fallow. For every stalk there were nine sprouts. It was a magnificent harvest.

From such a bountiful harvest, even after enough was set aside to eat for three years, there was still a surplus. They loaded the extra into their boats and took it to Nagasaki Island to sell. Nagasaki, a region in Japan with some thirty thousand households, was experiencing a severe famine at that time. The inhabitants were in desperate need, so the sale of the surplus produce brought in a total of one million *ryang* in silver.

Having made this tremendous profit, Hŏ returned to the island. With a sigh, he observed, "Well, it seems I have completed the test." He called together all two thousand men and women on the island and addressed them as follows:

"I had planned to come to this island with you and first of all provide a comfortable living. Then I intended to make up a new alphabet and teach it to you, then have new clothes made. In short, I meant that you should have comfortable lives. But this island is too small and my virtue too slight. I plan to leave. Make sure that you teach your children to hold their spoons in their right hands, and always let your elders eat first."

He then burned all the boats on the island. "Nothing goes out, nothing gets in," he said. And of the million *ryang* obtained in Nagasaki, he threw five hundred thousand into the sea. "When the ocean dries up, someone will find it. In our native land, it would be impossible to use up a million *ryang*. How much more so in this tiny place?" Finally, as he made ready to sail back to the mainland, he took on board all those who knew how to read. "Now I have removed the source of all troubles," he observed.

After leaving the island, for a time Hŏ went around the country providing aid to those who were in need but had no way to voice their distress.

When there was finally just one hundred thousand left, Hŏ said, "I'll pay back the rich man," and returned to Seoul. He found the rich man's house again, and looking in asked, "So, do you remember me?"

Pyŏn was very surprised to see Master Hŏ. He said, "I see your face isn't any better than before. I suppose that means you have lost the money?"

Hŏ laughed and answered back, "It's people like you who try to improve their faces with what they own. But what can even ten thousand do to put flesh on the bones of virtue?"

Hŏ turned over the hundred thousand. "I apologize," he said. "I couldn't bear the hunger, and I had not finished my reading. That was the time when I asked for your money."

Pyŏn was astounded. He got up and bowed to Hŏ, insisting that all he expected in the way of interest was 10 percent, or a thousand. Hŏ became furious at this. "Do you take me for nothing but a merchant?" he exclaimed, and walked out.

Pyŏn could not think of a thing to say. It was all most unusual, he thought, and silently followed after Hŏ. He watched him go into a thatched-roof hut down by South Mountain. An old woman was washing clothes in the stream near the place, and Pyŏn went up to her and asked who owned the hut. The old woman replied, "That old place is Master Hŏ's. He was very poor, but he liked to read things. One day, though, he just up and left. It's already five years since then. His wife is all alone. She figures he must have died somewhere far from here, so she does the memorial service for him every year on the date that he went off."

Having learned at last what Hŏ's name was, Mr. Pyŏn returned home, sighing as he went. The next day, he went back to Hŏ's house with the hundred thousand in silver, but once again Hŏ refused. "If I had wanted to be a rich man, would I have thrown away a million and kept one hundred thousand? But if you are willing, take the money and let me rely on your help. Send us food when we need it, and cloth to make the clothes we wear. I would like to live my life in such a fashion. Who really would want to trouble their minds with possessions?"

No matter what he tried, Pyŏn realized he would never be able to change Hŏ's mind, so from that moment on he made Hŏ's circumstances his first priority. If things became a bit short, Pyŏn himself would make sure that Hŏ had enough. But if he happened to bring any extra, Hŏ did not like it. He would ask Pyŏn, "What are you trying to do? Ruin me?"

But if Pyŏn happened to bring along some wine, Hŏ was very pleased. He would urge Pyŏn to share it and would drink until he was tipsy.

So things went for several years, as the friendship grew deeper between the two.

One day, Pyŏn asked conversationally, "How did you happen to make so much money, a million *ryang*, in such a short time, less than five years?"

Hŏ explained the secret of his success. "This will be easy to understand. We do not conduct trade with other countries by boat, and we don't use wagons or carts, so everything gets produced and used inside our borders. A thousand *ryang* is not a lot of money and you can't buy all there is of anything with it, but divide it into ten parts and one can buy a sufficient amount of ten different kinds of things. If the goods are light, they are easy to carry, and even if one of the ten products fails, the profits on nine will be enough to stay out of danger. This is how the peddlers go about it. But with ten thousand, you can buy all there is of anything. Just load it all in a cart, or a boat. Whatever there is in any area, you can scoop it all up at once, as if you were using a net. Now there are all kinds of things produced on land and all kinds of things that come from the sea, just as there are any number of things that can be used for medicines. Buy up all there is of anything. If it all falls into the hands of one person, no one else will be able to lay a hand on it. This is a sure method for making huge profits, but it causes tremendous harm to the common people. In the future, if some government official somewhere tries to make use of my method, it will cause the country great harm."

Pyŏn asked another question. "How did you know that I would give you ten thousand *ryang*?"

Hŏ replied, "It's like this. You are not the only one who could have given me ten thousand, and anyone with ten thousand would have. I even thought that I could probably make that amount of money on my own, but fortune lies with heaven, doesn't it? How could I know for certain that my greater plan would be successful? But someone who was ready to believe in me and my plan, that would have to be someone who already had good fortune. Since heaven provides well for those who are well provided for, wouldn't they realize they should give me the money? And since I was then using the good fortune of the lender when I used his money, naturally enough, I succeeded. If I had tried to do it on my own, there is no way to know whether I would have succeeded or not."

Pyŏn came to appreciate Master Hŏ's resourcefulness and ambition, and one day began to speak to him about other matters. He observed, "These days, there are not a few illustrious persons who wish they could cleanse the national disgrace of the Manchu pillaging of South Mountain Fortress. This truly is an objective for which such persons would join together and dedicate their best efforts. How can you, then, a person of real ability, be content to stay on the outskirts, hidden away and uncommitted?"

Hŏ replied, "For ages now, haven't there been any number of talented individuals who passed from view without a trace? Take Cho Song-gi. He was sent as an emissary into enemy lands, and yet grew old and died a commoner. Yu Hyŏng-wŏn distinguished himself in military procurement, but now spends his time on the sea coast. Can't we infer from this the lack of discernment among those who are responsible for state affairs? Or my case. I am good at business, and the money I made could have bought the heads of nine kings. But I threw my wealth into the ocean because there was no way to make real use of it here in this land."

Having heard Hŏ's reply, rising as it did from a deep sense of indignation, Pyŏn could only heave a long sigh as he returned to his own home.

Mr. Pyŏn had long been a close friend of Minister of State Yi Wan. Yi was serving, at the time, as commander of military affairs. He and Pyŏn were talking about this and that, when Yi said, "Have you run across anyone of real ability among the middle class? Someone who could take on a most important assignment?" Pyŏn proceeded to tell him all about Master Hŏ. The minister listened to the story with increasing interest. "Most remarkable! Can there be such a person? What is his name?"

Pyŏn replied, "I have spent time with him now for some three years or more, but I still don't know his first name."

"He must be a real genius. Take me to meet him, will you?"

That night, Yi left his retinue behind and went with Mr. Pyŏn for a visit, just the two of them. The minister waited outside the gate while Pyŏn went inside and explained why the minister had come. Master Hŏ seemed not to be listening, but instead said to Pyŏn, "Here, let's have some of that wine you brought. How about a pleasant cup or two?" He held out the cup for a drink. Thinking all the time about Minister Yi waiting outside by the gate, Pyŏn was too agitated to enjoy the drinking. Though he looked at Hŏ from time to time and mentioned the minister, Hŏ did not respond but went on talking about one thing or another. Only when the night had become late did he say to Pyŏn, "Why don't you invite him in, then?"

Minister Yi entered the room and offered his greeting to Master Hŏ with great deference, but Hŏ did not rise to greet him in turn. When Minister Yi eventually started into a lengthy explanation of his search through the country for an able person, Hŏ put up his hand and said, "The night is short but your speech will be long. It would be most tedious to hear it. What is your position now?"

"Well, I am serving now as commander of military operations," Yi replied meekly.

"So you have the full confidence of the state, I assume? What if I were to suggest that you request the king go to the hut of a person like the Chinese sage, someone I can recommend? Could you get him to go three times, as the Chinese king did?"

The minister listened to Hŏ's question, then bowed his head and replied, "This might be difficult. Can you make another suggestion?"

"I don't have another suggestion," Hŏ replied.

Minister Yi asked him again, an earnest entreaty.

"Well, then. Chosŏn owed a great debt to Ming China, long ago. After the fall of the Ming state, many of the sons of the Ming generals came to our country and have been living in great hardship, little more than wanderers, since then. Could your intercession make it possible for them to marry some of the women of the royal house? And could you arrange to take away a few of the big estates for them to live on?"

Once again, Minister Yi listened to what Hŏ had to say, then bowed his head and said, "This too might prove to be difficult."

"Well, if this is too hard and that is too hard, just what could you do? There is one thing, very easy indeed. Shall I tell you?"

Minister Yi's ears pricked up at Hŏ's reference to something that was easy to do. "I would like to hear about it."

This is what Master Hŏ said.

"Generally speaking, if one wants to make a name for oneself in the world, one has to make connections with intrepid men. And if one is planning to mount an attack on some other country, it simply cannot be done without first using spies. To be more specific, we know that Ch'ing all of a sudden seized control of everything. We also know that they have not been able to win over the Chinese people, but because Chosŏn accepted tributary status long before most other countries, Ch'ing does not regard us as anything much to worry about. Well then, let us select some of the young people of our country to go and study and find positions, as Silla did with T'ang long ago, and Koryŏ with Yüan. Then if we petition Ch'ing to allow our merchants to cross their borders, they will be pleased at Chosŏn's desire to establish closer ties. They will surely grant permission. Then let us cut the hair of our young people and have them put on Manchu dress. Our scholars can take the examinations for the foreign bureau, while the commoners go far into the southern regions below the Yangtze River to do business. They can examine the situation, and by making connections with intrepid men, they can plan to restore all things to the way they were and cleanse the national honor. If a descendant of the Ming royal house cannot be found, then someone else of suitable ability can be chosen to become the head of the state, as has happened before in history."

Minister Yi listened to Master Hŏ's articulation of this bold and comprehensive plan, but his reply was rather dispirited. "The illustrious officials these days all adhere very carefully to established etiquette. Who among them would want to cut their hair and put on Manchu-style clothing?"

Almost before Minister Yi had finished speaking, Master Hŏ rose up in a fury and shouted, "So this is what these so-called illustrious officials amount to? They are born on barbarian lands, but then they call themselves illustrious officials? Why, it is all nothing but mad pretense! That stuff they wear? Why, it's all so plain, from the coats down to the trousers, it's nothing more than mourning clothes. And their hair, the way they wear it long and piled up in lumps, it looks like those barbarian mallet heads! And what are they talking about, with this decorum they seem so devoted to? Pŏn O-gi of long ago, didn't he give his own head in order to avenge a personal wrong? And King Muryŏng was not ashamed to wear the clothes of the Manchus in order to strengthen his country. What is more, you say you want revenge for what happened to Ming, but then you tell me it would bother you to cut your hair! You would have to ride a horse, wield a sword, stab with a spear, shoot with a bow and arrow, throw stones, and still you won't change from those cumbersome, wide sleeves on your robes? Is this etiquette? Is this the decorum you want to preserve? I provide you with three comprehensive plans, and you tell me you can't try even one? Is this what it means to be a trusted official? Why, I ought to kill you!!"

Hŏ glared around from side to side, as if he were looking for a sword to grab and use on the spot. Minister Yi was scared out of his wits. He jumped up and dove out through the back window, running for his life to get back home. The minister spent the whole night thinking about how he had considered himself prepared. He went back the next day, but Master Hŏ had already disappeared. All that remained was the empty house.

PART 2

Negotiations in Korean Literature

INTRODUCTION

The three essays that comprise the second section of this book are not, I should say at the outset, a chronological study, although they do take their texts in a sequence that runs from the thirteenth-century *Samguk yusa* up to the seventeenth-century "Fisherman's Calendar" by Yun Sŏn-do. Neither are they a study of causation, of progress or decline, nor of great works or great authors. If anything, they are about articulations of a literary culture.

Several years ago, in a project focused on the struggles over authority and power reflected in a number of Korean literary texts, I made use of the concept of a human ecosystem from Elizabeth Perry's *Rebels and Revolutionaries in North China, 1845–1945*. Her account of struggles over material goods during periods of famine in China seemed translatable from economic history to literature.[1] The concept of the human ecosystem was most useful, it seemed to me then, in enabling one to consider the literary system as a whole and to trace within it the ways in which various groups accumulated the "wealth" of cultural literacy and made it difficult for others, no matter how they struggled, to gain access to it. The Chinese-language and culture-based state examination system in Korea was one key example. The *yangban* elites had both the time and the resources to study the Chinese language and the Chinese classics that formed the basis for the examinations, and made sure that this system remained the only route to status as an official, which in turn barred the nonelites, both lower classes and women, from access to power and authority in Chosŏn Korea.

I have continued to find the concept of literary culture intriguing. It is a human ecosystem, with finite resources, patterns of use and distribution, tension between the haves and have-nots; a monetary system, with discrete entities having certain ascribed values, where perhaps a little something in Korean might be exchanged for something else entirely in Chinese; but above all, a cultural system through which contending, competing, sometimes complementary forces interact. To what end? Is there some consistent purpose to all the activity, all the texts, all the inscribing and erasing? To present oneself in as favorable a light as possible; to look marvelous; to seem to be a king, or at least to be in charge at the moment? Or if that is not possible, then just to get away from it all?

It strikes me, as I consider these texts again, how great an optimism seems to inhabit them, a recurrent sense that with just a bit more of this or less of that, all will be right. The threatening spirit will depart, the new dynasty will settle into peaceful order, the quotidian details of one's place in the world will trace a meaningful path through life; or the massive displacements of foreign military, economic, or political intrusion will be held at bay long enough for the growth of Korean capacities to engage them. There is daring in these disparate texts, the courage to confront, even to provoke the dragons, and there is yearning for calm, for peace, for wholeness.

CH'ŎYONG AND MANGHAE TEMPLE:
A PARABLE OF LITERARY NEGOTIATION

INTRODUCTION

Ch'ŏyong and Manghae Temple, one of the stories in the Koryŏ monk Iryŏn's *Samguk yusa,* has attracted an astonishing number of scholars and other readers. As Cho Tong-il put it in a recent article, the story is like a mirror in which scholars seem to discover their own likenesses looking back at them.[1] I must confess to a twenty-year fascination with the story, which started with my reading of Ha Tae-hung's translation.[2] Like many readers, I imagine, I was intrigued by the images in the *Samguk yusa* (SGYS) of Korea in the Three Kingdoms and Unified Silla periods, images made all the more intriguing by the compiler's deliberate focus on folk materials, legends and myths, supernatural powers, spirits, and dragons. These were not at all the conventional elements found in accounts of the Koryŏ and Chosŏn periods in the official histories.

The next step in my reading of the SGYS was an article by the late Chŏng Pyŏng-uk published in the *Encyclopedia of Korean Cultural History, Han'guk munhwasa taegye,* in which he followed the approach that Marcel Granet had used in his study of the *Chinese Book of Odes,* the *Shijing,* to show that beneath the surface of the narrative were vestiges of an earlier culture, and that the songs in SGYS might have been parts of rituals in that culture that had little or nothing to do with the prose narrative context in which they were embedded.[3]

Much of the interpretive energy in the various publications about the story of Ch'ŏyong has been directed toward explaining Ch'ŏyong's strangely passive response when he returns to his home, after a late-night excursion, and discovers that his beautiful wife is in bed with someone, or something, else. All of these readings have been prompted by a Korean cultural projection in which the passivity of the "hero" seems dissonant within the context of the heroic narrative of Korean history.[4] Such readings—those, in any event, that focus on the character of Ch'ŏyong and his actions—seek to explain away, within different interpretive frameworks, the passivity of the final couplet in Ch'ŏyong's song: "Once upon a time that was mine; / what shall be done, now these are taken?" I shall argue that it is logically impossible to do this with models that are themselves constructed from the narrative identity of that character. Rather than being about what "Ch'ŏyong" "did," the story can be read as the negotiation of an exchange of both massive and finite dimensions. A switching of male and female roles is one aspect of the exchange; isolating it, showing how the narrative instigates it and at the same time leaves it uncompleted and therefore accessible to analysis, forms an interpretive framework that will make quite different sense of the famous final couplet. I adapt a model of cultural exchange from a recent study of classical Greek society and literature to shore up that framework, for I am persuaded that beneath the mirror of Ch'ŏyong's story, the narrated world is not at all what it seems.

THE "PROBLEM" OF CH'ŎYONG'S CHARACTER

Why does Ch'ŏyong dance and sing, rather than attack? Why the passive resignation of the last two lines of the song? The students in classes that have read the story, and other audiences, all know how *they* would have responded: a fight, a weapon, or at least angry words. Korean readers as well are puzzled deeply by the story, especially because the Ch'ŏyong character has become something of a culture hero. The *Ch'ŏyong Dance* and the *Song of Ch'ŏyong* were performed during Koryŏ times, as recorded in the *Akhak kwebŏm*, or *Primer for Music Studies* (1493), and were reconstructed in 1923 for official Korean cultural performances under the Japanese colonial occupation.[5] How is it that such an important element of the Korean national cultural heritage, a "representative" of the period of the Silla kingdom, of the Koryŏ era and culture, of one of the earliest surviving Korean historical narratives, and of modern cultural performances could be so weak? Several published accounts of the story and the song have tried to account for the perceived discrepancy.[6] Chŏng Pyŏng-uk wrote

that in his confrontation with the spirit, Ch'ŏyong evinces a degree of restraint that was deemed exemplary in traditional Korea.[7] Ch'oe Ch'ŏl argues that restraint was a type of behavior valued by the generations of
Buddhists who had passed the story along until it came to the Buddhist
monk Iryŏn, who added it to his miscellany.[8] Others associate the restraint,
or passivity, with a broader cultural decline in the later Silla period, during and immediately after Hŏn'gang's reign. In his article, Cho Tong-il
first summarizes the great variety of readings developed by other scholars,
then goes on to argue that the story is really about the early traces of a
drama tradition, and that the king was traveling to the various regions
and incorporating local drama traditions into court ceremonies in order to
strengthen the political relations between the central government and the
regional powers.

   In addition to these broad cultural interpretations, Ch'ŏyong's behavior has also been explained by claiming that he is a shaman; that the beautiful woman is someone with a serious illness; and that the song and dance
are actually a curing ceremony in which it would be dangerous to threaten
the cause of the illness, the powerful spirit.[9]

   Each of these cultural/historical readings addresses the "passivity
problem," but none questions whether Ch'ŏyong's behavior is actually as
passive as they take it to be. They are even less satisfactory when viewed
against the story in which Ch'ŏyong's little tale is embedded. How are the
king's actions to be balanced with Ch'ŏyong's? If Ch'ŏyong demonstrates
restraint, what virtue does the king personify? If Ch'ŏyong's song seems
passive and weak, how is it able not only to free the woman from the spirit's attentions but also to protect the people of the kingdom from future
intrusions by the spirit? And while Ch'ŏyong's provocatively passive behavior leads to such a beneficial outcome, how is it that the king, growing
increasingly lethargic and passive himself, presides over a kingdom that
ends in plain ruin? Or is there no connection to be drawn between the
two stories?

   Against the reading of Ch'ŏyong's character as a shaman, it is at first
more difficult to object. After all, shamanic curing ceremonies do proceed
more or less as described in the story, even today; it would have been in-
conceivable for the shaman to threaten the spirit; and the king seems to be
engaged in similar spirit-summoning activities. Yet the integument of such
a reading begins to show holes. There is a certain logic and sequence to the

king's excursions, accidental as his encounters with the spirits then seem to be. He first is to be found at Kae'unp'o, on the coast, east of the capital city of Kyŏngju. Later he travels to South Mountain, then north to Diamond Pass; finally he remains at the center, the fifth direction, at the palace banquet. Might these be part of a deliberately planned series of journeys? If so, of what kind? Ch'ŏyong, however, seems to be all accident. He goes out, comes back unexpectedly, and discovers his wife in bed with the human-shape spirit. While the king was taught his song and dance by spirits—or the people in the provinces—that he encountered, where did Ch'ŏyong learn *his*? Is it the same song and same dance as he performed with his father and six brothers to honor King Hŏn'gang?

NEGOTIATING PERSONAL AUTHORITY

Various forms of authority are claimed, negotiated, and asserted in the story. The king orders rest for the travelers on their excursion by the sea; he requests an interpretation of the fog, and orders a temple to be built when he learns it is a manifestation of the dragon; he confers office and wife on Ch'ŏyong; he alone is able to see the dances of the spirits and perform them, transmitting them to the human world. The king's authority depends, in every case, upon some prior or simultaneous condition or event: he sets out on the royal progress to the coast in order to get there, and once there, responds to the fog; his actions draw their rationale from their immediate circumstances, as for instance in the dances, where he and the artisans who carve the forms of the dance act as a recording device or a medium through which the invisible representations of the spirit world are made visible to the human eye.

Authority seems to be secured through negotiation and exchange. The king journeys to the shore where he stops to rest, and the dragon king manifests itself in the sudden fog; the king orders a temple built, and the fog breaks up; the dragon king, in exchange for the temple, sings and dances, then sends one of his sons back to the capital. Once the scene has shifted back to the capital, the king offers Ch'ŏyong a wife and a government office in exchange for his loyal service; he contracts for his domestication.

The authority acknowledged at each of these points is contingent upon the goods and services rendered. If, for example, the king's party had not encountered the fog, the story would have ended as the tale of a picnic; if the king had ordered a temple built without first obtaining the soothsayer's reading of the fog, Sea View Temple, otherwise known as Bridal Room Temple, would not have been established for the dragon; and so on. (Compare with SGYS III:4, where King Pŏphŭng is unable to have a temple built on the basis of his wishes alone.[10]) After the temple for the dragon is established, what second-order conditions follow? The temple marks a connection between the contingent authority of the king who ordered it built and the dragon for whom it was established. For the dragon king, the temple marks the gate through which his seventh son is sent away in the king's retinue; for the son, the temple marks a spot from which to "gaze at the sea" (the meaning of the temple's name), that is, to look back at the realm—figurative or literal—from which he came, but to which he cannot presumably return, given the negotiations and contracts by which he has been made a member of the king's retinue. The temple stands at the threshold between the world of humans and the world of the spirits, marking authority in a directional or valenced way: human on the one side, spirit on the other.

The irruption of the spirit into the Ch'ŏyong story shows the disruption, the disorder, that follows upon the abrogation of the terms of the distinction between the inner, private space of the home and the outer, public space of the city. Away from the house, the sign of his domestication, Ch'ŏyong creates a space into which the spirit world intrudes. Metaphorically re-placing Ch'ŏyong—or rather, creating a permanent *sign* of his presence, the gate plate, which is the domestic counterpart to Gaze-at-the-Sea Temple—closes that space, and the spirit promises—*contracts*—to honor Ch'ŏyong's actual and symbolized presence. Ch'ŏyong's presence, inscribing the details of the story immediately preceding, thus defines his domestic authority, establishes the order of the household, and secures the safety of the Silla capital.

NEGOTIATING LINGUISTIC MEANING

Just as various objects in the story become signs of the king's, Ch'ŏyong's, and others' negotiated authorities, the events of the story give meaning, through narrative authority, to place names such as Port of

Opening Clouds, to ceremonial dances such as the Frosty Beard Dance, and to locations that combine a narrative and ceremonial meaning such as the temple. In a less obvious way, the story also concerns itself with the question or issue of linguistic meaning in the exchanges between the king and the soothsayers regarding the fog, the meaning of the various spirits' dances, and the meaning—adduced by the narrator—of the unusual words sung by the mountain spirit in its last-ditch effort to warn the court of the dangers approaching. *Linguistic meaning* in all these instances, like personal authority, is contingent, defined in terms of the events or conditions surrounding the word, the phrase, the building, the dance, the song.

The story is also about a different type of linguistic meaning, one that is less obviously contingent but is nevertheless negotiated, or bartered. A recently published concordance to the SGYS lists forty-four occurrences of the word *mi*, the Chinese character for *beautiful;* three of these occur in the story of Ch'ŏyong. (Eleven occur as part of the name of a Silla prince, Mihae, in Book I, the story of King Naemul.[11]) As we shall see, the meaning of the word is absolute in the sense that it is not defined by conditions or events but in fact defines conditions and instigates events.

The first instance of the word is adjectival, preceding *woman, nyŏ,* to make the phrase *beautiful woman, wang i minyŏ ch'ŏ chi* 王以美女妻之; "the king by means of a beautiful woman wifed him" (Ch'ŏyong). The next instance of the word, immediately following, is as a verbal noun, *ki ch'ŏ sim mi yŏksin hŭm mo chi pyŏn wi in* 其妻甚美 疫神欽慕之 變爲人; "this wife so exceeded in beauty, the smallpox spirit adored her, changed into human form" (then went to her room at night and slept with her). Finally, after Ch'ŏyong has discovered the woman and the spirit in the bed, has danced and sung the song, the spirit resumes its true form, bows to Ch'ŏyong, and declares that because Ch'ŏyong has not displayed anger at what has happened, it "deeply feels and (holds) beautiful his action": *kam i mi chi* 感而美之. In acknowledgment of Ch'ŏyong's restraint, the spirit promises never to enter a house that has even a likeness of Ch'ŏyong displayed on it.

In the story, to *wife* Ch'ŏyong is analogous to giving him a government office: it is a contractual arrangement, in exchange for which the king expects to keep Ch'ŏyong's loyal service. We must infer that the woman has been chosen for her beauty, and thus pre-identified as a suitable offering to Ch'ŏyong, who is himself not human. Just as the house does not confine Ch'ŏyong, who habitually, we may again infer, goes out at night to celebrate in the bright moonlight, the marriage contract fails to confine the woman's exceeding beauty, which catches the attention of the powerful spirit. Beauty, in other words, binds Ch'ŏyong, through the body of the woman, to the king; and in a peculiar sense, that same beauty in that same body binds the spirit to Ch'ŏyong. To release itself from its guilt, the spirit, appropriately, returns *beauty* to Ch'ŏyong in acknowledgment of his restraint.

The etymology of the Chinese character *mi* uncovers a further layer to this tale of semantic circulation. The character is a combination of the written characters *yang*, or *sheep*, and *tae*, *large:* 羊 + 大 = 美. The historical meanings of the character range from *beautiful* to *pleasing* to *good* to *delicious*, deriving from the association of the character with the sacrificial offering of a large sheep, which the spirits would have been hoped to find delicious, pleasing, and in a broad sense, beautiful.[12] Ch'ŏyong's wife clearly is beautiful, and Ch'ŏyong's dance, pleasing. Together, they would comprise a pleasing offering to the spirit, which, in its confession to Ch'ŏyong, admits that it *desired, sŏn*, the beautiful woman. *Sŏn* shares the etymological root *yang* with *mi: yang* 羊 + *yŏn* 次, *drool* or *salivate* = *sŏn* 羨, *covet* or *desire*. Thus, the story about Ch'ŏyong, the beautiful woman, and the spirit can be restated as a semantic formula in which *beauty*, in the body of a woman, evokes its precise verbal cognate, *desire*.

GENDERING AUTHORITY

Most commentaries on the story of Ch'ŏyong declare the existence of a "problem," *munje*, in the final line of the song—"What shall be done, now these are taken?"—and then attempt to explain why or how Ch'ŏyong could have acted in such a passive, weak fashion. Because the commentary focuses on Ch'ŏyong, much of it inevitably concludes by obliterating or erasing him, turning him into a metaphor for Silla, a personification of the decadent age, or the like. The difficulty with Ch'ŏyong-centered efforts to explain his character flaws seems, though, to originate outside the text in the response to his action, in an overidentification of the reader with the character, whether as an individual—"*I* would never let that happen to *my* wife!"—or as a cultural representation—"*Koreans* don't let such things happen." But the story remains (relatively) clear: Ch'ŏyong discovers his wife in bed with another, but instead of taking some forceful action, he draws back, sings, and dances. If we look again at the narrative, we find that Ch'ŏyong's reaction is exceedingly effective when judged in terms of its implications for the Silla kingdom: the spirit agrees to go away and never come back. The spirit's agreement, furthermore, is not merely a private arrangement with Ch'ŏyong, but so widely known that the people of the kingdom come to use Ch'ŏyong gate plates to protect their homes from misfortune and to invoke blessings. Ch'ŏyong's action, or more broadly, the story of Ch'ŏyong, the spirit, and the beautiful woman, turns out to have had substantial benefit for Silla. It might be argued that the story is about Silla and its condition rather than Ch'ŏyong and his. The framework of this reading, which is not centered upon Ch'ŏyong, may in turn make possible a decentered reading of the final line of the song that will resolve the "problem."

Creating the problem and a possible resolution from the character and action of Ch'ŏyong requires the assumption that he acts, one way or another, on the basis of his personal and individual intentions. The various explanations create their problem by substituting the reader's identity for Ch'ŏyong's in considering the sudden discovery of four legs in the bed. They assume or suppose this is a moment calling for individual and decisive intervention. Why does Ch'ŏyong at that moment choose a decision path that *no one else* would? The story implicitly asks this same question when the spirit expresses wonder that Ch'ŏyong does not show anger. But is Ch'ŏyong free at that moment in the story to choose an individual and decisive course of action? In an obvious sense, being constrained by the narrative itself, he is not. Nevertheless, within the confines of the narrative the spirit is caused to marvel, while outside, the reader is caused to problematize. The reader's and the spirit's points of view coincide here: assuming the story is "about" ordinary life makes Ch'ŏyong's action seem extraordinary.

There is nothing in the story, however, that is ordinary life. It begins with what appears to be a simple description of life in the prosperous and happy kingdom. As with its modern counterparts, the housing development of the Silla kingdom had spread from the capital to the sea, and there was not a single thatched roof, a clear sign of economic prosperity. Music could be heard everywhere. The explanation in this remarkably compact account, in which almost every word seems vibrant with both meaning and significance, appears in the final clause: the wind and rains were in harmony with the four seasons. For an agricultural economy, the weather is more than just a pleasant attribute of a resortlike setting; it is the reason for prosperity. The warming winds of the spring come when they should, and the rains follow in the proper interval to ensure a productive harvest. The opening of the story, in other words, tells us that the Silla kingdom's economic well-being was due to the proper cosmological order of the four seasons.

The story goes on to describe how the proper seasonal order was maintained: by the ceremonial, directional excursions of the king. Tomb paintings such as the blue dragon on the eastern wall of Tomb 1, Chinp'ari, and other Koguryŏ tombs represent the association of the directions with colors, creatures, and auspicious influences.[13] King Hŏn'gang's various travels are in fulfillment of ceremonial obligations to the deities in the east, north, south, and center. (Perhaps the omission of the west is significant.)[14] In its two parts, separated by Ch'ŏyong's story, the account of Hŏn'gang's excursions also describes a gradual shifting of the activities associated with the ceremonies—singing and dancing, drinking and feasting—from the ritual to a profane context. With that shift, and the consequent recontextualization of the king's actions and the spirits' apparitions, the meaning of the dances and songs was misinterpreted. The king's ceremonial actions, according to the opening of the story, protected the kingdom and ensured its prosperity, but those same actions conducted in the profane context led to the kingdom's collapse at the end.

If Ch'ŏyong's action does have a beneficial effect upon the entire kingdom, it may be reasonable to suppose that it too is rooted in ceremonial performance, rather than being an unpremeditated, individual action. We know, to begin with, that Ch'ŏyong has performed songs and dances before, as part of the praise-ceremony for King Hŏn'gang. The story also tells us that the woman chosen to be Ch'ŏyong's wife is beautiful, and the usage of the word *mi* suggests, in turn, that her beauty has special significance as a guarantee of Ch'ŏyong's service, the impetus for the spirit's actions, and so on. Beyond or beneath the narrative, furthermore, the suggestive etymology of the word *mi*, especially in its etymological association with the word *sŏn*, the spirit's *desire*, would urge a "ceremonial" reading of the story in parallel with the supposed ceremonial nature of the etymologies. The ceremonial contextualization of Hŏn'gang's actions establishes a framework that also accommodates the story of Ch'ŏyong, the beautiful woman, and the spirit. That is, if we read the king's actions as being parts of a series of ceremonial performances, then we can also read Ch'ŏyong's actions as part of a ceremony, intended to protect the kingdom from the spirit while also engaging its paradoxically powerful, beneficial influence over other events. Ch'ŏyong's words and actions would be as circumscribed as the king's when *he* encountered the fog and asked rhetorically what it was.[15]

The narrative circumscription of Ch'ŏyong's character may be inferred from the problem of his supposed restraint; it is also implied, as suggested above, by the king's actions in giving him a wife and a position in government. What, though, of the beautiful woman? Why, for a start, is she such a cipher? Compared even to the problematically passive Ch'ŏyong, she is inert, completely lacking in specificity of any kind; yet in her beauty she is extremely powerful. How could such a figure become so entirely helpless, even granted that her husband is away? How could a king, though obligated to exercise his authority, simply choose such a person to be another's wife? What did he or the story offer in negotiation for her beauty?

I read the term *beautiful woman* as a sign, like the gate plate and the temple, a linguistic marker beneath which the particular woman and *women* in general are made to vanish. Henri Maspero described a woman like her in *China in Antiquity* in the following way:

> Calling the spirits was a rather lengthy business. The sorceress first purified herself by washing her face with water in which orchids had been boiled, and her body with water perfumed with iris; and then she donned magnificent robes, probably those of the deity she was calling. When the sacrificial offerings were ready, she sent her soul to find the god and bring him back with her to take part in the sacrifices. . . .
>
> Between the sorceresses and the gods, relations seem to have been complicated by a genuine love interest: it was the beauty of the sorceress which attracted the god and made him choose her.[16]

There are a number of indications that someone like the beautiful sorceress who would have shared a narratively equivalent role with Ch'ŏyong has been rendered one-dimensional, has in effect been reduced to a point. The narrative that links the etymology of the word *mi* to the word *sŏn* sacrifices the one to the other: beauty and the beast, the woman sacrificed to the spirit in the story; beauty and desire, the particular woman who was Ch'ŏyong's wife sacrificed to the male-centered narrative; inherent and contingent authority, the shamanic religious practices in which women played the leading roles—and men were assistants—subjugated to the imported Buddhist and Confucian practices of subsequent centuries in Korea, between late Silla, when the story is said to have taken place, and late Koryŏ, when it was written down.

The catalogue of King Hŏn'gang's excursions, starting with the compact but clear opening sentences of the story, establishes the deliberate, ceremonial nature of all of his actions. This narrative in turn suggests that the story of Ch'ŏyong, the beautiful woman, and the spirit could be read within a similarly deliberate, ritual context. Ch'ŏyong and the woman would both be bound to a predetermined response to the spirit's trespass. The *beautiful woman* might thereby be recovered from her role as a mere vanishing point in the narrative.

But what about the song's final line? A ritual recontextualization of the story may provide yet another explanation for Ch'ŏyong's restraint, but does it also explain the woman's inert condition or the spirit's remarkable proposition? Hŏn'gang's part of the SGYS story concerns the ceremonies to ensure the prosperity of the kingdom by propitiating the directional deities, ceremonies at which Hŏn'gang was simply the authority figure presiding at that time; he was *the forty-ninth king*. Likewise, the "Ch'ŏyong story" is not about a culture hero named Ch'ŏyong, but instead describes a ceremony designed to propitiate a deity having great powers of a more general sort that can be deployed for either harmful or beneficial purposes.[17] Who, though, presided at the ceremony? One line of argument, presented by the narrative itself and therefore naturally followed by readers, places Ch'ŏyong at the center, in the controlling position. All the particulars of the story fit nicely into this reading, except for the apparently accidental nature of the encounter between Ch'ŏyong and the spirit. Such a melodramatic plot twist is a thin thread from which to hang the general well-being of the people of the kingdom. It also does not accord with the deliberate, ceremonial nature of the king's actions—or rather, the deliberate nature of the king's actions, once identified, argues that the Ch'ŏyong part of the story should be read in the same way.

Yet because the "problems" continue to multiply with Ch'ŏyong at the center no matter how the interpretive context is manipulated, and also because the narrative itself provides signs that the woman's identity has been erased, there is reason to suppose that the beautiful woman might have been the center of the story, the one who actually presided over the ritual. If she, the *sorceress* of Maspero's description of Chinese ritual practice, were returned to her original status, the story might be retold as follows:

> Hŏn'gang's reign was a time of peace and prosperity. The proper rituals were performed, and the seasons followed one another in their proper sequence. But the people of the kingdom, despite their prosperity, continued to suffer the ravages of illness brought on by the spirit, a fearsome and elusive force.
>
> There lived at this time a powerful shaman woman, who knew that her spells and her beauty might enable her to capture this spirit and domesticate it. But she needed a strong and talented helper for the ceremony, which was bound to be dangerous for both her and her helper. Not just any old musician would do; she needed someone extraordinary.
>
> The king knew of her wishes and had an idea. He traveled to the eastern coast, performed rituals, had a temple built, and summoning the dragon king of the sea, explained the difficulty. Pleased by the offerings and the respect shown him, the dragon king answered, "My seven sons are all talented in music and dance. I shall have them perform for you, and you may call upon one of them to accompany you to the capital and assist your shaman woman in her plan."
>
> The sons danced and sang, and King Hŏn'gang watched them carefully. Finally, he said, "Please send the seventh son." The dragon king was saddened that his favorite son, the youngest, had been chosen, but a promise is a promise, and he sent him with the king.
>
> When Ch'ŏyong came to the house, the shaman woman greeted him and explained her plan. "I shall make myself beautiful, using perfumed waters and putting on my special robes. In this way I shall at-

tract the attention of the spirit. You must go out and wait, away from the place where I will be. Do not go too far, and do not stay away too long. To lie with me, the spirit will change into human form, and that is when we can capture it. That is the moment for you to return. No matter what you see, just sing the song that I will teach you, and dance."

Ch'ŏyong was confident and agreed to the plan. On the first night, the woman prepared herself carefully and Ch'ŏyong went out, but the spirit did not appear. The next night was the same, and the next. Ch'ŏyong became distracted, being young, and strayed away for a drink of delicious moon-bright wine. When he remembered himself and returned, the woman was furious. "It was here," she told him. "Do not make that mistake again."

Ch'ŏyong, abashed, assured her that the next night he would be on time, and he was. Ch'ŏyong returned to the house with a great retinue of musicians and others, saw that the spirit was there, and sang the riddle song that the shaman woman had taught him.

> Under the bright moon of the capital
> I enjoyed the night until late.
> When I came back and looked in my bed
> there were four legs in it.
> Two are mine,
> but the other two—Whose are they?
> Once upon a time that was mine;
> What shall be done, now these are taken?

The spirit knew that it was caught. There was no escape, and the saucy threat of the last line of the song was only too clear: the song meant *its* legs, and that Ch'ŏyong and the powerful woman could do whatever they wished with it. In order to escape this humiliating situation, the spirit bowed down between Ch'ŏyong and the shaman woman, saying, "Please, most gracious ones, extend your restraint to me. I have made an awful mistake, but if you let me go, I promise not only to keep disease from this entire kingdom, but to use my considerable power for the good of your people as well."

The shaman woman and Ch'ŏyong agreed, and thereby secured the well-being of the people of the kingdom.

LITERATURE AS NEGOTIATION AND CONTRACT

In addition to the numerous points of negotiation within the story of Ch'ŏyong about, for example, the meaning of fog, a place name, or the name of a dance, several other negotiations are also inscribed by SGYS. Noting them may suggest not only the specific qualities of SGYS as a Korean text, but also a more general model of written narrative as negotiation and contract.

When Hŏn'gang orders a temple built in honor of the dragon king, he requests a *sa*, a Buddhist temple within which the dragon king's recognition of the king's authority could be ritually celebrated and reenacted. The story effects an accommodation between the kind of ritual practices that occur at planned, calendrical intervals, appropriate for the propitiation of the directional/seasonal deities, and the ad hoc responses called for by a sudden fog, an illness, or other problems. Incorporated within this negotiation is the accommodation between the public sphere for ritual and the private. The temples, the pavilions, and the palace where the spirits appear at the end are public, established spaces for the conduct of ritual performances; the house and the room where the beautiful woman and Ch'ŏyong encounter the spirit are private spaces. In the design and layout of its grounds and buildings, the temple would have embodied a symbolic pattern that the priests would have incorporated in the performance of their ceremonies.[18] The structure of a house might also have some symbolic significance, but further, when a shaman visited the house with her or his costumes, implements, and noisy ceremonies to attract the spirits, the house would have taken on a specific, immediate ritual significance.[19]

The story of Ch'ŏyong also negotiates a massive shift in the ritual significance of the king's activities, from their proper performance and meaning at the beginning of the story to their dangerously self-indulgent licentiousness at the end. Iryŏn makes explicit that the latter led directly to the kingdom's downfall. The narrative does not make an explicit causal connection between the prosperous kingdom and the beautiful woman, but the following sequence of correspondences is suggestive. The opening sentences of the story describe a happy, prosperous kingdom, a beautiful and productive land. The kingdom enjoys its prosperity because of the rituals conducted for the various appropriate deities, but at the same time the kingdom's well-being might be expected to attract the envious attentions of malevolent, outside forces, human or supernatural. One such force is represented by the spirit, which, drawn to the beautiful woman, is also, by metonymy, desirous of the wealth enjoyed by the kingdom and its people. Thus the woman's actions to capture the spirit result in the practice and belief of the people of the kingdom, the *kugin,* in the efficacy of the Ch'ŏyong gate plate to protect them singly, household by household, and as a polity. Curiously, there is a further parallel between the woman and the country: both are *beautiful,* in a wide range of the meanings associated with that term, from attractive to pleasing, accomplished, productive. At the same time, both are surrounded by rituals and marked off by architectural and other signs that signify their reservation from outside forces or influences. The beautiful woman is to a certain degree defined by her selection as Ch'ŏyong's wife, by her being at home, by her attractiveness to the spirit; her beauty is a complex and disturbingly contradictory attribute, finally something to be admired and protected on one side of its semantic field, and desired and pursued on the other.

The story of Ch'ŏyong thus negotiates an array of complementary attributes, values, practices, meanings. These elements could be said to represent a synchronic image of Silla society and culture. The story also tells of the historic shift in context, from sacred to profane, of the ceremonies performed by the king. This shift recapitulates or compresses a diachronic view. Another major shift underlying the events of the story is what might be called the creolization of Korean culture and language, that is, the displacement of native terms and practices by Chinese. Here I am referring not to the translation of Korean stories into Chinese written form, although that is surely a part of the process, or result; rather, the story presents the on-site, ad hoc, nonsystematic substitution of Chinese words and phrases for Korean names. The features of the Korean physical and cultural landscape are being renamed in Chinese: Port of Opening Clouds, Sea View Temple, Frosty Beard Dance, Form Examination. All of these names are Chinese, each of these places is defined by an event that happened there in the historical narrative of the story, and all are made uniformly generic by their mode of definition. Any place by the sea where the clouds parted could be named Port of Opening Clouds, any temple with a view of the ocean could be named Sea View Temple, and so on, including any woman, who could be *beautiful*. Each Chinese name marks a turning point in the story, a shift from one realm, for example that of the spirits, to another, such as the human; or from sea to land; or in the case of the woman, from the king to Ch'ŏyong and from Ch'ŏyong to the spirit. These names also mark points of transformation, from spirit to human, invisible to visible, male to female, Korean to Chinese. Like Ch'ŏyong's gate plate, they also have a valence, marking inside and outside, and they signify restricted access: only by conducting the proper associated ritual or by recognizing the associated meaning can one pass from one side to the other.

Finally, the story itself comprises a valenced sign of transformation. It is about (or accomplishes) the vanishing of Korean specifics under (or through) the sign(s) of Chinese-language generalities. The story is a contract for the disappearance of one set of elements—Korean vernacular—into another—Chinese. The SGYS and the stories it comprises mark the end point in a process of negotiation between two languages, the "original" Korean in which the stories and songs circulated and the literary Chinese in which the monk Iryŏn wrote them down.

THE CLASSICAL MOMENT

Repeated and intensive reading will disclose the negotiations that a text has momentarily concluded. A text also engages historic, cultural changes. In the case of the SGYS, these include the complex changes that took place between the time of Hŏn'gang's actual reign, 875–886, and Iryŏn's writing of the SGYS in the late thirteenth century, as well as those that followed, including the construction of the nationalist historical narrative for modern Korea that now seems to demand an explanation of the Ch'ŏyong problem. The narrative fate of the *beautiful woman* raises a more general question, whether such cultural negotiations require, somehow, the marginalization of women. For a comparative example I shall turn to a recent study of a similar process of negotiation in the development of classical Greek literature.

Gail Holst-Warhaft has argued in *Dangerous Voices: Women's Laments and Greek Literature* that the (roughly) seventh- to sixth-century B.C. development of the Greek city-state, with a standing state army and codified laws, necessitated the control of women's laments and the cycles of revenge they had instigated. Women's laments were banned by Solon and in their place appeared the funeral oration, conducted in state-centered rather than personal, family, or village terms, and the theatrical manipulation of themes of revenge in such plays as Aeschylus's *Oresteia.* Holst-Warhaft summarizes this process as follows:

> To say that the state was acting in its own interests in restricting women's roles at funerals is not to legitimize the laws passed by Solon, but rather to confirm that the new social order at Athens and a number of other city-states in the classical period involved, even necessitated, the careful control of women in their prominent role as mourners of the dead.[20]

In the name of a new political order in Greece, women's laments were identified as a source and example of disorder—this despite the fact, as Holst-Warhaft points out, that women's laments were in fact carefully controlled, artistic presentations, whereas men's laments were uncontrolled.[21] Something of the same contrast between order and disorder can be discovered in the story of Ch'ŏyong. For example, ceremonies conducted in a ritual context by definition have order and therefore intelligible meaning, whereas the same ceremonies conducted outside the ritual context in a spirit of play have neither. The nontrivial nature of the distinction is seen in the association of order and meaning with the health of the body politic as described in the opening sentences of the story, and the disorder and licentiousness at the end that lead to the downfall of the entire kingdom.

Holst-Warhaft's analysis of the mutual implication of social-political change with literary expression provides an elegantly powerful model. Its power derives from the author's primary focus not on gender relations *per se* or on social structure, though both are clearly implicated in the model; nor even on literature in its broadest sense, but specifically and pointedly on the unique powers of song.[22] The Athenian city-state legally banned women's laments not because they were sung by women, but because the songs were powerful instigators of social action.[23] With that venue of expression closed down, the songs reappeared in such dramatic works as the *Oresteia* as the dirges and laments that recur throughout the trilogy, until finally their persistent recurrence is blocked and the cycle of revenge they propel is ended by the sophistry of Apollo's argument that women are not blood relations to their children.[24] Apollo's speech, in which the craftiness of the argument is almost too obvious, addresses the proposition that the killing of one's mother—Clytaemnestra by Orestes—is a lesser crime than the killing of one's husband—Clytaemnestra's murder of Agamemnon. If one can accept the initial premise, that a woman is "no parent of that which is called / her child, but only nurse of the new-planted seed that grows,"[25] then the cycle of revenge can be ended.

The final contractual detail to be cleared up in the play is the fate of the Furies, the Erinyes, who had pursued Orestes, demanding vengeance for the death of Clytaemnestra. At the end of the play, Athena offers the Furies a proposition that, evidently, they find impossible to refuse: in exchange for canceling their plan of revenge against Orestes and their further threat to devastate all of Greece, they will be rewarded with the grateful devotion of the citizens of Athens. As Holst-Warhaft succinctly puts it, "The last play of the trilogy extends the identification of female power with monstrosity to its dreadful limit, then attempts to contain the horror it has unleashed by turning the witches into good fairies, the Erinyes into the Eumenides."[26] The transformation is excruciating to observe.

> *Chorus (of the Furies):*
> Gods of the younger generations, you have ridden down
> the laws of an elder time, torn them out of my hands.
> I, disinherited, suffering, heavy with anger
> shall let loose on the land
> the vindictive poison
> dripping deadly out of my heart upon the ground;
> this from itself shall breed
> cancer, the leafless, the barren
> to strike, for the right, their low lands
> and drag its smear of mortal infection on the ground. . . .[27]

Athena answers them with the logic of participatory democracy, the legal system, ballots:

Listen to me. I would not have you so grieved.
For you have not been beaten. This was the result
of a fair ballot which was even. You were not
dishonored, but the luminous evidence of Zeus
was there, and he who spoke the oracle was he
who ordered Orestes so to act and not be hurt.
Do not be angry any longer with this land.

. . .

In complete honesty I promise you a place
of your own, deep hidden under ground that is yours by right
where you shall sit on shining chairs beside the hearth
to accept devotions offered by your citizens.[28]

Though the Furies resist, eventually they allow themselves to be persuaded.

Chorus:
Lady Athene, what is this place you say is mine?

Athene:
A place free of all grief and pain. Take it for yours.

Chorus:
If I do take it, shall I have some definite powers?

Athene:
No household shall be prosperous without your will.

Chorus:
You will do this? You will really let me be so strong?

Athene:
So we shall straighten the lives of all who worship us.

Chorus:
You guarantee such honor for the rest of time?

Athene:

I have no need to promise what I cannot do.

Chorus:

I think you will have your way with me. My hate is going.

Athene:

Stay here, then. You will win the hearts of others, too.[29]

The final scene of the final play in the trilogy is eerily similar to the confrontation among the beautiful woman, Ch'ŏyong, and the spirit. Good order, domestication, veneration, and respect are negotiated and contracted, and then sealed with a marker—the gate plate in the story of Ch'ŏyong, and the sign of the hearth in *The Eumenides*.[30]

I argue not only that this model is applicable to a comparison of ancient Greek and Korean textual materials but further, that literature in more general terms can be thought of as implicated in cultural negotiations and contractually structured to conclude those negotiations, if only temporarily. Such a model needs to include the particulars of what is being negotiated, the parties involved, and what their stakes in the negotiations may be. The model shows, in Greek tragedy, traces of the negotiations surrounding the establishment of the city-state vis-à-vis the village and family social organization of the preclassical period, and in the story of Ch'ŏyong, various strands of political, linguistic, and gender negotiation and contracting.

Korean culture is not alone in marginalizing women in its narratives about itself. As Carol Pateman begins in *The Sexual Contract:*

Classic social contract theory and the broader argument that, ideally, all social relations should take a contractual form, derive from a revolutionary claim. The claim is that individuals are naturally free and equal to each other, or that individuals are born free and equal. . . . Contract theory is not the only example of a theoretical strategy that justifies subjection by presenting it as freedom, but contract theory is remarkable in reaching that conclusion from its particular starting-point . . . the doctrine of natural individual freedom. . . .[31]

As Pateman argues, however, the revolutionary idea of individual freedom upon which the social contract is constructed rests, in turn, upon a key assumption:

> The contract theorists also insist that men's right over women has a natural basis. Men alone have the attributes of free and equal "individuals." Relations of subordination between men *must*, if they are to be legitimate, originate in contract. Women are born into subjection. . . . The fact that "individuals" are all of the same sex is never mentioned; attention is focused instead on different conceptions of the masculine "individual."[32]

It may be cold comfort, or none at all, to view Korean culture as participating in an apparently universal marginalization of women; and in any case, it is not my intention here to argue that Korea's history reveals a greater or lesser degree of animadversion on women. I am concerned with an idea of literature as a process of negotiation, and interested in the results of approaching particular literary works as partial contracts. This seems to me an especially productive course to follow with a work such as the story of Ch'ŏyong, which is so full of terms relating to negotiation and acts of contracting that they seem almost to bubble over the edges of the narrative. I propose that the narrative represents the negotiation of a positional exchange between the man and the woman in the story. The man is brought forward and marked by the gate plate that bears his likeness, while the woman is sent back into the interior of the house, turned into a passive cipher. She becomes no more than two *other* legs in the bed, two *other* legs in the lines of a riddle song, her vanishing marked by the word *beautiful.*[33] Under the terms of the linguistic and cultural spell that banished her, we are left with the so-called puzzle of the final line of the song and Ch'ŏyong's seeming passivity.

If the woman is returned to the powerful role she once performed in religious ceremonies, however, the puzzle of the final line is resolved. The vanishing of the woman and the puzzle of the final line are linked by a complex of interwoven narratives. All the elaborately epicyclic theorizing about Korean cultural and institutional history cannot resolve that puzzle as long as the male figure remains at the center of a cosmological system and narrative that is rightly centered upon the female. The puzzle of Ch'ŏyong's song seems to be a trace of the reordering of the relationships among the woman, the man, and the spirit. The next chapter considers the implications of the reordering process for the writing of a history.

SONG OF THE DRAGONS FLYING
TO HEAVEN: NEGOTIATING HISTORY

It is possible to give a concrete and detailed analysis of any utterance, once having exposed it as a contradiction-ridden, tension-filled entity of two embattled tendencies in the life of language.[1]

INTRODUCTION

In the middle of the fifteenth century, the fourth king of the Chosŏn dynasty, Sejong (1418–1450), ordered the composition of a song to praise and celebrate the founding of the new dynasty. *Yongbi ŏch'ŏn ka, Song of the Dragons Flying to Heaven,* described the actions of the dynastic founder, Yi Sŏng-gye, reign name T'aejo (1392–1398); his son Pang-wŏn, the third king (T'aejong, 1400–1418); and their four ancestors at the end of Koryŏ and beginning of Chosŏn. The song sketches the story of the gradual movement of the Yi family from their home in the southwest, in the city of Chŏnju, up to the opposite end of the peninsula and then down to the capital, from which Yi Sŏng-gye went out in the 1380s to win distinction as a military commander in campaigns against the Japanese pirates along the southern coast, and against rebellious tribes in the north. The *Song* asserts directly that it was not personal ambition but a response to the will of heaven and the wishes of the people that led General Yi to assume control of the state. The *Song* describes the signs, portents, and many ancestral deeds that foretold Yi Sŏng-gye's eventual accession to control of the state; highlights the efforts of T'aejong, the third king, to solidify his hold on the throne and succession; then closes with a series of stanzas admonishing the future Yi descendants to remember, when seated comfortably on the throne and surrounded by all the accoutrements and temptations of office, the difficult trials their founding ancestors endured.

To some degree, the *Song* has been slighted in Korean histories of literature. It is esteemed as the first official occasion for the use of the new Korean alphabet but criticized for being, like other examples of the *akchang* verse form in which it was composed, overly didactic.[2] Yet the individual components as well as the overall structure of its argument are elegantly crafted and assembled. The *Song* turns history into prophecy and registers the transition from the Yi family's initial struggles to establish and stabilize the dynasty to the ongoing ceremonial and administrative tasks required to maintain it. For all the seeming directness and simplicity of its argument, the *Song* is a complex hybrid of intertwining histories and languages. This chapter explores these component features and pursues the argument that the *Song*, like the *Story of Ch'ŏyong* examined in the preceding chapter, incorporates certain negotiations toward a desired goal. As the final fifteen stanzas become explicitly contractual in nature, they flourish history as a sign, like Ch'ŏyong's likeness, to bind the future rulers of the Chosŏn state to behavior that will continue to fulfill the purposes of their ancestors' actions.

HISTORY AS PROPHECY

The first two stanzas frame the overall project of the *Song* by asserting the cosmological significance of the change in dynasty.

> Haedong's six dragons rise in flight,
> their every deed heaven's gift,
> the sign the same as the Ancient Worthies.[3]

According to Chinese-language annotation attached to this, as to every stanza, *Haedong* is a customary term for Korea, meaning "East of the (Yellow) Sea" or "East of Parhae," Parhae being the remnant of the earlier Koguryŏ kingdom. The six dragons are Yi Sŏng-gye, his son the third king Pang-wŏn, and their four ancestors. The first line and its annotation state that the six founders are a manifestation of the first hexagram, *ch'ien*, described in the Chou book of divination, known as the *Book of Changes* or

Yijing. All the lines in the hexagram are unbroken. The dominant fifth line, the "governing ruler of the hexagram," according to the *Book of Changes,* indicates "Flying dragon in the heavens, a great man will appear."[4]

That fifth line would correspond neatly to Yi Sŏng-gye, the fifth member of the Yi family to be mentioned in the opening stanzas and the actual founder of the dynasty. Interestingly, the *Yijing* interprets the unbroken line at the top to mean "Arrogant dragon will have cause to repent," and warns against "titanic aspirations,"[5] a reading that could easily have been applied to Pang-wŏn, Yi Sŏng-gye's politically astute and thoroughly ruthless son. The second line of the stanza asserts that each action—*il mada*— of the six dragons/ancestors also constitutes a sign of heaven's blessing, while the third line states that the process of signification described in the first two lines about Korea's recent history is the same as that which marked the rise of the ancient Chou dynasty (c. 1027–236 B.C.) in China. The first stanza also initiates the song's structural pattern of pairing a Korean historical event with a Chou Chinese counterpart.

The second stanza restates the prognostication about the long life of the new dynasty as metaphor:

> The tree with deep roots does not tremble in winds;
> its flowers are perfect, its fruit abundant.
> Waters rising from deep sources do not end in drought;
> forming a river they flow on to the sea.[6]

The opening phrase, "The tree with deep roots," has become, in effect, the modern Korean-language counterpart to the Chinese *Haedong* to mean the Korean people and nation. South Korean President Park Chung Hee used the phrase for his New Year's calligraphy in 1974, and it has in the decades since spread to the commercial realm in South Korea as well, as a name for a wide range of products and companies.

The cosmological claim of the first stanza, reworked into the metaphors of the second, is translated one last time in the third and fourth into the human narrative that will follow the Yi family ancestors and dynastic founders up to stanza 109:

> The King of Chou residing at Pin Valley
> there began the works of empire.

Our ancestor residing in Kyŏnghŭng
there began the works of the kingdom.

When he ventured among the barbarians
and the barbarians came to threaten,
he moved to Lofty Mountain,
and this was part of heaven's doing.
When he ventured among the Jurchen
and the Jurchen came to threaten,
he moved to Virtue Source,
and this was part of heaven's doing.[7]

There are several observations to be made about these two stanzas. For one, the stanza about the founding ancestors, the King of Chou and "our (Korean) ancestor," reiterates the stanza immediately preceding, for it describes the roots of the family tree that then grows throughout the balance of the song. Kyŏnghŭng, the city named in the third stanza as the ancestral home of the Yi family, was former Kongju, in the southwest. This was an area particularly mistrusted by Wang Kŏn, the founder of the Koryŏ dynasty, and the city was destroyed on his orders. The third stanza seems to suggest that whatever "our ancestor" (Mokcho, great-grandfather of Yi Sŏng-gye) had been doing in Kyŏnghŭng, simply by being there he was initiating the (new) kingdom that was to become the Chosŏn dynasty. How did Mokcho's presence in that place set in motion the downfall of one dynasty and the triumph of the next?

Kyŏnghŭng was an important town in the southwest, singled out and destroyed by Wang Kŏn at the time of the founding of Koryŏ. The *History of Koryŏ* contains an intriguing passage regarding the fate of the southwestern region. The relevant section is the eighth of the ten injunctions that Wang Kŏn announced to his followers shortly before his death:

In the territory south of the Ch'aryŏng Mountains and beyond the Kongju River, the shapes of the mountain ranges and the features of the terrain are disordered. The character of the people of that place is likewise disordered. If they should manage to work their way into government or marry into the royal family and seize political office, they will bring turmoil and disaster to the country. Or in their continuing resentment at Paekche's incorporation into the unified kingdom, they might demonstrate their feelings and cause disturbances along the routes of royal processions. . . .[8]

Wang Kŏn had ordered the destruction of the city of Wansan, in North Chŏlla Province, in 936. Rebuilt, it was later known as Chŏnju or Wansan, in the Kyŏnghŭng area mentioned in the *Song*. Kyŏnghŭng had in turn been known as Kongju, the region mentioned in the Eighth Injunction. The history of the various names of the regions where the family lived and the sequence of their moves from one to the next, including the beginning of the whole story in a quarrel over the affections of a *kisaeng*, is described in maplike detail in the annotation to the third verse.[9] The subsequent story reads like an overlay of the family narrative on that verbal map, much as the account of King Hŏn'gang's reign, in the *Story of Ch'ŏyong*, marked out the various ritual directions and key locations around the Silla capital.[10] The Yi ancestors had thus started their series of heaven-intended actions leading to the overthrow of Koryŏ and establishment of Chosŏn, the "works of the kingdom," from precisely the politically and geomantically charged area that Wang Kŏn had predicted would be a political threat and that he had destroyed, in rather uncharacteristic style, in a vain attempt to uproot that threat. The Yi family thereby fulfilled the prediction of the injunction by their deeds, as described in the verses that follow in the *Song*, beginning from the mere fact of their residence in the area. Having its beginning in Kyŏnghŭng, in other words, gives the story of the Yi family's moves from one place to another the significance of a human prophecy being fulfilled.

The project of compiling and writing the *History of Koryŏ*, *Koryŏ sa*, in which the injunctions were recorded, was initiated during Yi Sŏng-gye's reign, but the history was not completed and published until 1451, four years after the *Song* itself was produced and one year after Sejong's death. For both the *History* and the *Song*, the work of compilation was carried out by a single group of scholars, one of whom, Chŏng In-ji (1396–1478), wrote the prefaces for both works. We know from Chŏng's preface to the *History*, furthermore, that Sejong put Chŏng in charge of the project at a fairly advanced stage with orders to correct it, and that the compilers under

Chŏng's direction consulted with the king on all matters concerning the "basic direction" of the *History*.[11] Thus it seems reasonably clear that Sejong took a direct interest in both projects, and that in some way he intended to bring the two stories, one about Wang Kŏn's founding of Koryŏ and concerns about his dynasty's historical longevity, the other about his own family's parallel accomplishment and concerns, into some form of mutual confrontation.

This concern with events in Korea's recent past seems particularly significant with regard to the actual founding of the Chosŏn state. The Yi family and their followers engineered the removal and murder of the last two kings of the Koryŏ state, son and grandson of a monk advisor to Koryŏ's King Kongmin, who was childless. They installed a collateral member of the Wang family, a relative of Wang Kŏn, only long enough to remove and banish him, thereby ending the Wang family's reign. In the maneuvering to finish Koryŏ and establish the new royal line, Yi Sŏng-gye's son Pang-wŏn, the sixth of the dragons celebrated in the *Song* and the father of Sejong, proved to be an adept and ruthless political figure. When Yi Sŏng-gye chose another of his sons as his heir, Pang-wŏn arranged the murder of the government ministers who supported that son, then murdered the son, his own half-brother, and another half-brother for good measure. Most notoriously, it was Pang-wŏn who assassinated the Koryŏ statesman Chŏng Mong-ju, whose loyal resistance against the Yi faction had become increasingly troublesome. This incident is recorded in the *History of Koryŏ*, and the treatment of the moment when Pang-wŏn reports the deed to his father makes it clear that the Yi rulers were concerned to clear Yi Sŏng-gye of guilt and ascribe Pang-wŏn's action to the motive of filial concern for his father's safety.[12]

The scene is translated in the section "Chŏng Mongju," from the Biographies section of the *History of Koryŏ* in the present collection. The key line, given to Yi Sŏng-gye, reads like a reply in a court of law to the question, "Did you kill, or did you cause to have killed, the Koryŏ statesman Chŏng Mong-ju?" Yi retorts: "You have gone off on your own accord and killed the minister. Do you suppose the people of this land will actually think that I knew nothing about it? You were brought up to follow the dictates of loyalty and filiality, but now you have dared to commit this most unfilial act!"[13]

Like Wang Kŏn before them, the Yi family evidently faced a residue of resentment at their actions. Against such feelings, the *Song* advances the initial argument that these deeds were all done in obedience to heaven's will. In the closing sequence of admonitions to future monarchs, the *Song* engineers a shift from historical description to ritual presentation as it maneuvers past the same difficult problem that beset the Athenian city-state. How does a state shift the actions of its citizens, who may feel aggrieved by greater or lesser perceived injuries, from direct retribution to obedience, however reluctant? More generally, how does the state bring order and control to situations of disorder or unrest? In ancient Athens, womens' laments, in recounting the circumstances of individual deaths, had prompted revenge against the parties responsible, leading to the endless cycles of violence that the *Oresteia* trilogy engages. The Athenian city-state banned the laments and deployed in their place the funeral oration, a generalized account of the glory of death in the service of the state.[14] As will be seen, the *Song of the Dragons* moves from depictions of the military and political exploits of the founders, against whom resentment might have encouraged the kind of counterplot that Wang Kŏn had feared, to a generalized portrait of the ruler as a ceremonial leader against which, or whom, no personal animosity could be directed.

There is, finally, a point about the meaning of a key word in the original fourth stanza that needs to be clarified. The phrase "heaven's *doing*" is difficult to translate because of its echo in the considerably altered context of stanzas 110–125, the admonitions to current and future monarchs. The original term is *hanŭl ŭi ttŭt*, the *ttŭt* of heaven. There are several ways in which the term *ttŭt* could be rendered, including "intent," "meaning," or "significance."[15] Thus, the early moves of the Chou king and of Mokcho could be read as "that which heaven intended"; that is, they were essential parts of the heaven-intended founding of the two dynasties. The phrases could also be read to mean that the actions were revelations of "heaven"; that is, of the operating principle of the universe. The matter is complicated by a distinction in the Chinese-language version of the stanza: in the case of the Chou king the phrase *ch'ŏnsim*, or "heaven's heart," is used, whereas for the Korean ancestor the phrase is slightly different: *ch'ŏn'gye*, or "heaven's opening" or "revelation." This point is explained in the Chinese annotation. *Doing* is meant to suggest that heaven caused the event to happen, and also that the event was a revelation of heaven itself.[16]

HYBRID NATURE AS A QUESTION OF MEANING

The term *ttŭt* is a key component in the *Song*'s overall argument, as it marks the reframing of historical narrative as prophecy. In the *Story of Ch'ŏyong*, a similar function is fulfilled by certain characters in the narrative. When fog appears, the soothsayers are asked to explain it; when a strange, four-legged apparition is found in Ch'ŏyong's bed, he turns aside, in a gesture resembling the way the narrator will turn out of character and address the audience during a performance of the *p'ansori*,[17] and asks, in effect, What is the meaning of this two-plus-two? At the end of the story, the narrator's voice is heard in the passage explaining the meaning and the significance of the strange message, *Chi ri da do p'a do p'a*, of the spirits' song. In the *Song of the Dragons*, individuated characters do not ask the question; rather, the text is filled with many different questions involving *ttŭt*, which provoke explanations from grammatical and vocabulary notes to historical allusions and cosmology.

A practical reason for the repeated emphasis on explication is that the *Song* is highly elliptical and allusive; its verse format summarizes and hints at the events it records, rather than describing and explaining them in such full detail as would be found in a history. The *Song* employs an effective pedagogic strategy by providing a discernible but not entirely clear verbal passage with each stanza. A reader can follow the passage, though it is elliptical in most cases and written in Korean—not Chinese—in all cases, but then is left with the question, What lies behind this? What does this signify at some deeper level? What is the meaning, the *ttŭt*? The meaning is given explicitly and repeatedly in the annotation at the end of each Korean verse, at the end of each Chinese verse, and then in summary annotation ranging from a brief paragraph to a lengthy essay that explains both together. The message is the same: just as the event in Chinese history was a sign of heaven's intention to change that dynasty, so too the event in recent Korean history was a sign that heaven intended the dynasty to change, and intended the Yi family to be the agents.

The *Song* is, in fact, a complex hybrid. With the exception of the second stanza and the closing sequence of admonitory stanzas, each stanza begins with a Chou Chinese historical example that is then paired with an event from the recent history of the Yi family and their rise to power. This feature of the *Song*'s composite structure has been noted in Korean commentaries addressing the question of whether or not it demonstrates Korean cultural subservience to China. Cho Tong-il, for example, observes, "There is the opinion that, because the Chinese example is always put first, (the *Song*) . . . shows a subservient attitude, but it would be more appropriate to say that it shows equality between the two." [18] Each Korean-language stanza is annotated in Chinese, then paired with a Chinese quatrain. It is entirely likely that the Chinese stanzas were the "originals," composed in response to Sejong's initial order but then translated into Korean as the concurrent alphabet project neared completion. Cho Tong-il offers one explanation for the inclusion of the Chinese verses: the rules of the new alphabet were not widely known at the time of the *Song*'s official promulgation and a literary Chinese version would, therefore, have been more accessible; he adds that another reason would have been the practice of rendering royal praise songs in the form of the poems in the *Shijing,* the Chinese *Book of Odes.* [19] To accompany each pair of stanzas, Korean and Chinese, extensive annotations in Chinese were prepared over the course of two years by a special committee appointed at Sejong's order in 1445. The final version of the *Song* is thus in the form of Korean-language verses followed by brief notes in Chinese, each stanza paired with a Chinese-language "translation" with its notes, and a final, extensive Chinese-language annotation on each stanza's historical background and references.

Most scholarly commentary on the *Song* and other less formal comment, such as the literary handbooks and the self-study manuals prepared for college entrance examinations, focuses primarily on the Korean-language verses. Even observations about the aesthetic qualities of the *Song* or its component parts tend to be couched in the same terms. In commenting on the widely known second stanza, which begins with the line "A tree with deep roots," one of the Korean literature self-study manuals observes, "Of all one hundred and twenty-five stanzas (stanza 2) . . . has the highest literary worth, the reasons for which are 1) the writing is entirely in Old Korean, 2) it shows novelty and suggestiveness in its deployment of metaphor, and 3) there is no reference at all to Chinese matters." [20] A reader might wonder if there was anything at all distinctive about the use of the Korean language in stanza 2; might observe that the stanza in Korean is, like all the others in the *Song,* accompanied by a Chinese translation with vocabulary usage note; and might infer a strongly felt need to find and claim Korean cultural independence behind the third point, "no reference at all to Chinese matters." This last point seems apropos with regard to Cho Tong-il's unusually balanced observation, mentioned above, concerning the nature of the relationship between the Chinese and Korean examples that each stanza presents.

As a major cultural icon, the Korean alphabet has overshadowed the *Song* in many ways. More specifically, the hybrid nature of the *Song* may be overlooked because of the present-day emphasis on the alphabet as a distinctly Korean *national* project. In the event, the alphabet was vigorously resisted by the scholar-official class until the very end of the nineteenth century, not least because it seemed likely to produce an unruly combination of Korean practice and Chinese theory in at least some levels of government as well as the society at large.[21] The *Song*'s complex mix of Chinese *and* Korean history, oral *and* written sources, Korean songs and stories transformed into Chinese-language stanzas and annotations, embellished with Korean and Chinese signs and portents, does not easily lend itself to the modern teleological narratives of growth toward Korean cultural independence. It might, in fact, serve as a textbook example of the contradictions, tensions, and embattled tendencies referred to in the head-note to this chapter.

To give some sense of the complex character of the *Song*, a translation follows of verse 15, in which the connection is drawn between the founding ruler of Koryŏ, Wang Kŏn, who fears the possibility of a threat to his rule originating in the region to the southwest, and the Yi family's destruction of Koryŏ and founding of their own dynasty, which fulfills Wang Kŏn's anxious vision. The Korean verse (translation in larger type) is followed in the original by the Chinese version of the same; each is accompanied by brief Chinese commentary and note (translations italicized). A summary of the historical annotation is also appended.

> Leery of the region south of the Yangtze
> he dispatched an envoy;
> but who could have blocked
> the rise of the Seven Dynasties?

Yangtze Prefecture is part of Chinju. The Yangtze River is in the southern part of the prefecture and forms the boundary between it and Chingang, in western Zhejiang. The envoy was, as below, a luminary.

Leery of the region south of the Kongju River
he admonished his descendants,
but were the Prophecies of the Nine Transformations
merely a human's doing?

The character kuk *here means* prophecy, *the* Prophecies of the Nine
Transformations *being the name of a book of prophecies collected in the
Spirit Annals. It states that the country's capital will be changed nine times,
and also that the founder will have received the mandate of heaven.*

Uneasy of the region south of the Yangtze
he sent an envoy,
but who was there to command
the Seven Dynasties to stop?

Stop *here means* verbal command.

Fearful of the region south of the Kongju River
he admonished his descendants,
but was the altering of the Prophecies of the Nine
    Transformations
a matter of man's intention?

Succession *here means* descendants.[22]

A lengthy summary of the Chinese historical background to the first
part of the stanza is followed by a description of the Ten Injunctions and
their historical background. The same general account of this part of
Koryŏ history can be found in a passage from the *Koryŏsa* translated and
included in the anthology section of this book.[23]

WARRIORS BECOME KINGS

The *Song* turns history into prophecy, and the past into the future
in that transmutation; the two, mutually inscribed, become the body of the
song. This is more than just a characterization of the local argument that

this text repeatedly articulates. Linked as they are in the successive stanzas, Chinese and Korean history also assume the relationship of *langue* and *parole*, the universal language of literary Chinese and the particular, Korean written statement. By distinguishing it, repeatedly marking the difference between it and Chinese history, the *Song* gives Korean history retrospective significance. The same formula seems to continue in the concluding stanzas, numbers 109–124, the admonitions to future monarchs. The paired structure remains the same, though with a Korean historical event, not a Chinese one, cited at the beginning of each couplet, followed by a reference to the present or future situation of the king on the throne, surrounded by court officials and confronting the difficulties not of pacification and establishing rule but of maintaining the monarchy. Each of the stanzas ends with the same phrase: "Do not forget the meaning and significance (*ttŭt*) of this (the earlier ancestor's deed)." With the significance of the Korean historical events related to the founding of the dynasty established in the first part of the *Song*, the admonitions project that significance forward, turning it into example. Stanza 112, for instance, draws a contrast between Yi Sŏng-gye's physical discomforts during his harrowing military campaigns and Sejong's dangerously comfortable situation as reigning monarch.

> Pursuing the work of the king,
> leading the army formations,
> many were the days, one after another,
> when he did not remove his armor.

> When you stand draped
> in the royal dragon robe
> wearing the belt of precious jade round your waist,
> do not forget his example.[24]

(Stanza 112)

For the stanza above, the annotation explains that the dragon robe and jade belt were gifts from the Chinese (Ming) emperor to the sovereign (*chŏnha*), who would have been Sejong. The image recorded in that stanza thus represents the Ming emperor's recognition of Sejong's status as the monarch and presentation of him to the world as king, designated or symbolized by the robe he wears. The robe itself is described in some detail in the annotation, which reads as a verbal portrait of a king defined, as it were, by the symbols of his office rather than by his or his ancestors' historic struggles to seize power:

> The emperor bestowed upon our ruler a dragon robe to drape his body and a belt decorated with precious gems. The dragon robe was three measures in size, woven with gold dragons. The head and right foreleg were on the front, the tail and left foreleg on the right shoulder, with the right rear leg on the back. The dragons around the hem were woven in gold, eight in front and eight behind. The belt was woven in the style of a sword belt, with a jade ring buckle. The belt was laced with red silk, with loops of yellow gold, decorated with red and green jewels in fine silk. Thus did the emperor bestow upon our monarch the dragon robe and jeweled belt.[25]

This is a formal portrait of the monarch, Sejong, as civil ruler. Of necessity, perhaps, given the exigencies of space within a stanza, or perhaps because of customary practice, the portrait is not a likeness of Sejong himself but of his kingly figure in the royal Ming robe. Divided between the reference in the verse stanza to wearing the robes and thus acting as king and the physical description of the robe presented in the annotation without the human wearer, this portrait functions rhetorically in much the same way as did the verbal map of Korea, sketched in the earlier part of the *Song* as a political and geomantic force field divided between Kyŏnghŭng and the capital. By their move from Kyŏnghŭng to the capital and their struggles along the way, the Yi family fulfills Wang Kŏn's anxious prophecy; by wearing the dragon robe, Sejong fulfills the meaning of his identity as king. The shift from descriptions of historical events, even in allusive or attenuated form, in the earlier part of the *Song* to a description of the size, pattern, and nature of the decorations of the king's robe in stanza 112 and its annotation signals the shift in attention from the functions of the ruler as military leader—the role fulfilled by the founder of the dynasty, his son Pang-wŏn, and their four ancestors, the six dragons of the *Song*—to the monarch's identity as ceremonial head of the state.

There are no surviving, original portraits of Sejong or other early
Chosŏn monarchs, so there is no way to trace the iconographic change
directly in Korean materials, but the contrast expressed in stanza 112 is
directly represented in Chinese art history by a parallel and contemporaneous shift in Ming royal portraits.

> The transformation, about the year 1500, of the Ming imperial image
> from a heroic warrior-king to an iconic representation in which the
> human dimension of the emperor all but vanishes behind a surfeit of
> ceremonial paraphernalia reflects the increasingly ritualistic and de-
> personalized imperial rule of late Ming China. While the early Ming
> emperors directed military campaigns, proclaimed laws, and managed
> the affairs of the state, the Hung-chih emperor, characterized by histo-
> rians as the most humane of the Ming rulers, personified the ideal ab-
> solute monarch precisely because his demeanor and implementation
> of imperial rule were passionless and impersonal. In his portrait he
> has become a ritual vessel; devoid of personality, he is the ultimate
> embodiment of the absolutist state. It is this new schematic representa-
> tion that would become the model not only for Ch'ing imperial court
> portraiture but for all later Ming and Ch'ing private ancestral por-
> traits.[26]

Like the *Song* itself, the portrait in stanza 112 is more complex than it
seems at first. The king is wearing the dragon robe, a gift from the Ming
emperor and a sign of that worthy's official, public recognition of the new
Chosŏn state some sixty years after its founding. Further, while the king
himself is addressed in the stanza, being urged not to forget the significance
of his ancestors' deeds, that admonition is then projected into the future
toward any and all successors who would put on the dragon robe. In its
negotiated effect, this moment in the *Song* seems structurally similar to the
confrontation in the story of Ch'ŏyong between Ch'ŏyong and the demon.
The demon pledges to stay away, but only on the condition that Ch'ŏyong
or his likeness, the gate plate, be there. The king in his robe, a gift that in
the annotation becomes an iconic representation, a likeness, of the monarch, is admonished not to forget the meaning, the purpose, the significance—*ttŭt*—of his ancestors' actions, which were intended for precisely

that moment. It will be the glory of the future rulers to wear the robe, but also their task to govern in the spirit of their ancestors and to conduct those rituals, such as the performance of the *Song,* whose purpose it is to reaffirm the pledge.

PERFORMANCE AND KOREAN *SIJO* VERSE:
NEGOTIATING DIFFERENCE

We have observed, in the first and second chapters of this section, instances of displacement and the interpretive gaps that they initiate. In the story of Ch'ŏyong, a beautiful woman, Ch'ŏyong's wife, is in effect made to disappear, reduced from a narrative figure with the same potential to act as Ch'ŏyong or the king to the dreadfully inert, passive point or position defined by the king's intentions toward Ch'ŏyong, Ch'ŏyong's toward the demon spirit, and the spirit's desire for her beauty. Her reduction to a one-dimensional point is marked by the phrase "beautiful woman," much as places, spaces, and ceremonial manifestations are marked in the story by Chinese place names or titles. The puzzling final lines of Ch'ŏyong's song can either open to the vast, infinitely regressive series of interpretive frames that recent commentators have provided, or be resituated in a cultural frame in which a beautiful woman acts as an autonomous individual. That frame finds a counterpart in Maspero's study of ancient Chinese civilization, and also in contemporary shamanic ritual practice in Korea.

The *Song of the Dragons Flying to Heaven*, with its placid, regular structure and abstract, emblematic historical references, displaces the violently contested history of Koryŏ's demise and Chosŏn's beginning. The dragon song also registers a series of linguistic displacements. The *Song* was the first official state use of the newly promulgated Korean alphabet; it registers, therefore, both a shift from the Chinese cultural and linguistic models—a negative register, as it were—and, simultaneously, a positive shift toward the new alphabet. The *Song* contractualizes the end point in a process of translation into Korean of Chinese-language verses that had been assembled from the Korean-language stories told by people in the southwest about Yi Sŏng-gye's military campaigns. In this displacement, Korean-language oral materials, the original stories, were turned into Chinese-language written texts; but as these were in turn translated into the Korean-language verses of the *Song*, they were put into a form that could be performed to Chinese ritual music. (As noted above, the performance of the *Song* at court used the Chinese-language verses, not the Korean.) The several stages in this process of appropriation, registration, and displacement are presented in the woodblock print edition, which places the Korean stanzas first, followed typographically by what the page arrangement makes Chinese-language "translations" of the Korean, even though very likely they were the Chinese-language "originals" produced by the officials commissioned to gather the songs and stories from the people. All are wrapped in the various kinds of Chinese-language notes and annotations.

The two songs, Ch'ŏyong's and the dragons', are deeply implicated in history even as they question and reflect it. They cannot be "read" outside of their historical contexts, but at the same time they instigate readings of their contexts as interrogations of history itself. Both songs, in the end, are riddles. Ch'ŏyong's asks, "What has four legs and yet occupies my bed?" The dragons' song poses an equally rhetorical question, "What could all these portents and historical precedents mean?" The songs, in effect, take all questions into themselves as they inscribe an even larger question, "What do we have here?" In the case of Silla culture, the riddle song can be read as the question, "What do we see, what do we have, when Korean culture is creolized by Chinese?" With *Song of the Dragons*, "What is the result when one dynasty displaces another?" In both cases, the complex response is tempered by the ceremony of dance and song, or the rituals of court music, costume, and decorum. Whatever the real situation, the historical moment, the presentation of the song involves turning away from it, avoiding a response that might otherwise begin from possessive resentment. Wang Kŏn's Eighth Injunction, as we have noted, addresses the same problem when it refers to the popular outbursts that might greet a ruler who traveled to the geomantically and politically unfavored southwest.

This third chapter turns to one of the notable literary forms of the Chosŏn period, the three-line verse form known as the *sijo*. Four *sijo* texts are considered: the Koryŏ statesman Chŏng Mong-ju's "Song of a Loyal

Heart," *Tansim ka;* the sixteenth-century *kisaeng* Hwang Chin-i's "Jade Green Stream"; General Yi Sun-sin's "Song on Hansan Island" from the evening of the final battle against the Japanese invaders in 1598; and finally, several verses from the *sijo* song sequence *The Fisherman's Calendar, Ŏbu sasi sa,* by Yun Sŏn-do, regarded as the epitome of the genre. As will be apparent, even this simple list of four "most representative" works from what might be thought of as a purely literary genre contains highly charged elements of Korean historical-cultural identity. Chŏng Mong-ju and Yi Sun-sin were historical figures, one killed, as we know, by political opponents, the other, as every Korean school child knows, by Japanese invaders. We shall find that their *sijo* are not simply literary texts, but neither are they simple articulations of historical events; they are hybrids of the two. These two most famous historical *sijo* texts also stand, in turn, in a sort of opposition to the other two, by Hwang Chin-i and Yun Sŏn-do, which apparently register no such historical moment. In that contrast, however, the four songs are also joined. If some *sijo* have evident historical significance or historical significance is ascribed to them, while others do not have such readily apparent importance, the latter might be said to be shaped by a deliberate choice to turn away from history—to leave government office, for example, and seek a meaningful life in rustic retirement, or to write about such a topic. If the choice to turn away from history is deliberate, then the history must leave its impression in the resultant *sijo*, and a reading will have to demonstrate where and how. But on the other hand, if there are forces at work—or at play—in the *sijo* genre that are non- or antihistorical, how might they affect the readings of those iconographic *sijo* songs by the statesman Chŏng Mong-ju and the admiral Yi Sun-sin? Are literary forces at work in the composition, transmission, performance, or reading of importantly historical *sijo* texts? If so, what are they? Are historical forces, cultural forces, ritual forces at work in what seem to be examples of purely literary *sijo*? Do *sijo* songs pose riddles, like Ch'ŏyong's song or the *Song of the Dragons*? Or, put somewhat differently, if a given *sijo* song is an answer, can the initial question be recovered from a reading of it?

Much of Korean classical literature was written in Chinese. Formal writing—histories, poems and notes on particular occasions, diaries and journals—seems until the end of the nineteenth century to have been produced in Chinese, while the informal side of life in Chosŏn Korea was expressed in the vernacular, in Korean. Younghill Kang's *The Grass Roof,* written in English and published in the United States in 1931, is an idealized portrait of traditional Korean culture drawn to show how modernization shattered it in the first two decades of the twentieth century; it describes instance after instance of this division: the established, calendrical occasions in the life of the village were celebrated in Chinese verses, while sudden outbursts of powerful feelings were expressed in Korean songs, either folk songs or *sijo.* Two examples:

> My grandmother stood at the door of the first room, with her
>   coat over her head, looking out into the night. In a low
>   voice that was more a wail than a song, she was singing the
>   old popular air:
> O how sorry I am! How sorry I am!
> The wind is blowing! The wind is blowing!
> The rain is dripping, the rain is dripping!
> O my poor child, where are you to-night?[1]

. . . .

> My crazy-poet uncle read us many New Year poems from the
>   Chinese. One of them was this:
> Under the inn's cold light, one man lies awake.
> Why does the heart of the wanderer unspeakably ache?
> He's a thousand *li* from home on New Year's Eve!
> Frost bites his beard, and a birthday comes at daybreak.[2]

This bipartite picture has a compelling explanatory quality: Korean culture can be viewed as both enabled and constrained by its Chinese elements. That is to say, the formal side of Korean culture can be said to have found both expression and authorization in Chinese language, philosophical writings, and literary forms, while an opposing Korean character and spirit kept trying to assert itself. This formula seems to have venerable roots. Wang Kŏn, the founder of the Koryŏ dynasty, somewhat cautiously notes the significance of Chinese culture in his Fourth Injunction: "from ages past our people have modeled culture and ceremonies on those of T'ang. But the two lands are different, and the people also are different. Do not be obsequious, trying to copy things exactly." But that statement may have been intended less as a critique of the true T'ang models than as disparagement of the Khitan rulers of China at that time, for it concludes: "The Khitan, who rule the land next to us, are nothing but a country of animals. The dress and institutions of such as they should never be taken as models."[3]

The inscription of Korean culture within the Chinese system of language left traces, as we have seen, in the *Samguk yusa*. The text itself, to start, was in Chinese; place names were newly coined in Chinese; and the story of Ch'ŏyong, like several others in the SGYS, registers a shift in gender roles, like the shift in place names: the beautiful woman, I have suggested, was displaced from her previously central position in ritual. The notable perplexity in modern-day efforts to read the song, in the story of Ch'ŏyong, the king's failure to hear properly and understand the warning of the spirits at the end of the story; or, in the story of Lady Suro, the husband's and the villagers' frantic reaction to her abduction—all mark points where indigenous ritual practices have been supplanted by male-centered ones. In these cases, the reader, like the perplexed villagers in the story of Suro, has to be taught how to interpret and then deal with the circumstances. Likewise, even in the *Song of the Dragons,* the audience is provided with a catalogue of the signs and portents for the end of the old regime while the case is constructed for obedience and devotion to the new one.

Like the alphabet project that it accompanied, the *Song of the Dragons* authorized the use of the Korean language in public matters as well as private conversation, a use that was vigorously resisted by Korean officialdom, quick to notice a threat to the Sinified system of study, preparation, and state examinations that they monopolized, for the next four hundred years. Wang Kŏn's Fourth Injunction, recorded in the *History of Koryŏ* produced at the same time as the alphabet and the *Song,* sounded a note of caution concerning the full baptismal immersion, as it were, of Korean national identity in the stream of Chinese culture. From various perspectives, all three projects express an explicit interest in the dynamic, shifting relationship between Korean and Chinese culture, including, especially, language.

THE DIVIDED REALM OF THE
LOYAL STATESMAN

The relationship between the Chinese and Korean languages parallels the division in Korean culture between the hierarchical, Sinified, Confucianized realm of the *yangban* elites and the horizontal, egalitarian, vernacular realm of the common people. In his study of Korean social structure, *A Korean Village: Between Farm and Sea*, Vincent Brandt described the bipolar axis of what still could be called "traditional" Korean society in the following terms:

> Two distinct ethical systems affect ordinary, everyday behavior. One is formal and explicit. It is largely lineage oriented and embodies a clearly structured hierarchical system of rank and authority that is closely linked with Korean aristocratic traditions, but that has a pervasive effect on village life as well, particularly with regard to kinship relations, personal status, and ceremonial activities.
>
> On the other hand, what I have called the egalitarian community ethic is informal and has no codified set of moral principles, although many aspects of it are expressed in proverbs and homely aphorisms. Important values are mutual assistance and cooperation among neighbors, hospitality, generosity, and tolerance in dealing with both kin and non-kin. Resistance to authoritarian leadership outside the family is combined with strong in-group solidarity for the natural community, defined as a society in which everyone knows everyone else, and where people interact more frequently with one another than with outsiders.
>
> In this scheme a highly ranked, prestigious, formal ethic is confronted by a vulgar egalitarian tradition that embodies many features of what is often called tribalism. Both ideologies are an integral part of the cognitive orientation of each villager.[4]

This model of Korean social structure is useful in illuminating Korean literary works as well, and the relations portrayed within them. Ch'unhyang, the heroine of the *Song of Ch'unhyang*, to cite a prominent example from the *p'ansori*, oral narrative repertoire, embodies both aspects. She is the daughter of a *kisaeng*, or professional woman entertainer, of a class situated at the lowest end of the Confucian social scale; at the same time, she is the daughter of the government official who had the liaison with the *kisaeng*. In accord with her mother's upper-class aspirations, Ch'unhyang has been well educated in the Chinese classics, but to Mongnyong, the upper-class Romeo who later pledges his love to her, as well as to the new governor who attempts to force Ch'unhyang to become his mistress, she is just a pretty *kisaeng* girl. "Can't I have a look if she's a *kisaeng*'s daughter? Go summon her," says Mongnyong to his manservant. Eventually, under Ch'unhyang's tutelage, Mongnyong becomes more egalitarian in matters ranging from the sexual to the philosophical. The corrupt and stubborn new governor of the province, however, after trying to use his position, bolstered by repeated references to the Chinese classics, to force Ch'unhyang to abandon Mongnyong, in a final rage sentences her to a ritualized beating, then imprisonment and death.[5]

The principle for which Ch'unhyang is portrayed as being willing to die, and for which she recites a list of historical exemplars—interestingly divided between other Korean *kisaeng* recognized, with public memorials, for their fidelity and Chinese statesmen renowned for their refusals to abandon one regime when it was supplanted by another—is itself articulated around a private versus public axis of loyalty to one master: "We are told that a faithful subject will never serve a second king, while a married woman will never care for another man." The principle is expressed in the Chinese-language phrase *ilp'yŏn tansim*, "single-hearted devotion," or literally, "one piece red heart."

When Ch'unhyang is flogged for her recalcitrance, at the counting out of the first stroke of the wooden paddle on her legs, picking up the theme of *one* for the first stroke, she translates the phrase from a moral, political principle to a domestic one:

> Single-hearted devotion meaning
> a firm heart faithful to one husband. . . .[6]

The famous *sijo* song ascribed to Chŏng Mong-ju uses the phrase in its conclusion:

> Though this body die
>   and die and die again,
> white bones become but dust,

                        a soul exist, then not,
              yet this single-hearted devotion to my lord:
                    How could it waver, ever?

The phrase *ilp'yŏn tansim* in modern Korean is a common synonym for *sincerity* or *devotion*. It would be interesting to be able to trace its historical usage, to discover the extent of its provenance in the vernacular. There are several other *sijo* songs that use the phrase. Chŏng Pyŏng-uk's *Sijo Dictionary,* for example, includes four others, which range from a *sijo* (#17) very much like Chŏng Mong-ju's in being ascribed to a political martyr, Pak P'aeng-nyŏn (1417–1456), to an anonymous drinking song (435) and a love song (82) rather similar to Ch'unhyang's declaration of devotion.[7] A CD-ROM search of the Chosŏn dynasty *Veritable Records* reveals that the phrase was not recorded until the mid-sixteenth century, during the reign of King Myŏngjong (r. 1545–1567).[8] Chŏng Mong-ju's *munjip,* or collected writings, include what is generally said to be a Chinese translation, *hanyŏksi,* of his *sijo* that uses the phrase *ilp'yŏn tansim.*[9] Yet because the *munjip* was assembled and published by Chŏng's sons in 1439, nearly fifty years after the death of Chŏng Mong-ju, while the vernacular *sijo* song was not recorded in written form until the eighteenth century, it remains impossible to decide which version of the song was the original and which the translation, and difficult to feel certain about the ascription of the *sijo* to Chŏng Mong-ju.

The very broadness of the scale of representation, the generality of the phrase in current linguistic usage and the modes of its transmission in the classical works cited—Chŏng's *sijo* song is among the best known of all *sijo* and Chŏng himself is the exemplar of absolute loyalty, while the *Song of Ch'unhyang* is the "best loved" of all Korean traditional tales, with the character of Ch'unhyang a symbol for perfect womanly devotion—suggest that the phrase might well be considered an element of an oral tradition, and further, that the Chŏng Mong-ju *sijo* might itself be thought of as part of that oral tradition. The emblematic but clearly fictional nature of the *p'ansori* character Ch'unhyang suggests that the appropriate way to read the story and the song about Chŏng Mong-ju might be as part of an oral tradition of stories and song, not history. The *Koryŏ sa*'s account of Chŏng Mong-ju's death does not, in fact, mention any song, nor the supposed exchange at the banquet with Pang-wŏn.[10]

Thinking of the *sijo* in terms of an oral rather than a written literary tradition reminds us that all such songs have their accompanying stories. If they are considered in a broader performance context, like *p'ansori*, as existing with implied scripts that in turn require fictional authors as characters, we can distinguish between the literary character and the historical figure, between the subject of the Chŏng Mong-ju *sijo* song and the historical figure whose death at the hands of his political rivals is recorded in the *Koryŏ sa*. The "authors" of *sijo* in a doubled sense are liminal characters in "their" stories. They exist temporally between the song and its performance: the stories about them will be told before the performance takes place, as the story of Chŏng Mong-ju and Yi Pang-wŏn is taught before the *sijo* is memorized by Korean children in school; and they occupy places in formal, written, Chinese-language histories and literary collections on the one hand, and vernacular, performance traditions on the other. Like the place names and the titles of songs and dances in the story of Ch'ŏyong, *sijo* songs are valenced signs, traces of a subject's passing from one realm to the other, from *a* story to *this* story, from Chinese-language history to Korean story, and from the past of "once upon a time" to the present of performance.

LOOKING AWAY: THE ADMIRAL'S SONG

Richard Rutt, in his anthology of *sijo*, *The Bamboo Grove*, visits and revisits a famous *sijo* song by Admiral Yi Sun-sin. Rutt observes the song first as an example of the difficulties for literary history posed by the uncertainties of ascription, and in another section of the book he analyzes the Chinese phrase *ilsŏng hoga* in the final line of the song to describe the phonological effects that can be achieved by the insertion of Chinese phrases in the Korean literary song context.[11]

Moon-bright night on Hansan Isle,
    and I sit alone atop the lookout.
I hold my great sword by my side,
    and as my worries deepen,
from somewhere comes the single note of the Mongol flute,
    piercing to the very bowels.[12]

This *sijo* song is said to have been composed by Admiral Yi, heroic leader of the Korean defense against Hideyoshi's sixteenth-century invasion of Korea, on the night before the final battle with the enemy. Rutt's discussion of the song observes that the concision of the Chinese phrase *ilsŏng-hoga*—"a single note of the Mongol flute"—adds to the overall effect of the song. He concludes that such phrases "often have a marked emotional value, because they are frequently familiar or allusive. In this case the length of the vowels gives the phrase a heavy sound, heralding the end of the poem."[13]

To fill in around Rutt's observations about the Chinese phrase and how it works in the song, let us note that the third line begins with a common "twist" word in *sijo*, a turn toward some other direction of thought or meaning: *ŏdisŏ* means "from somewhere," and redirects the sense of the song away from the admiral seated on the wall to the empty distance surrounding him. The word also shifts the focus of the song from the immediately and physically perceptible to the indeterminate, abstract distance beyond sight, the realm of invisible sounds and anxieties. From somewhere out in that realm comes the single note of the flute. The *sijo* then literally reincorporates the admiral high up on the wall fortifications, hearing the sound.

The scene is exquisitely lonely, yet it also suggests a connection between the great admiral and the men he was to lead into battle against their enemies, the Japanese. The song is an accomplished one, and we might leave it with that much of an assessment. But the flute and its single note invite further attention. The phrase in the final line means "one note of the Mongol flute." The song takes on a deeper resonance when we recall that Mongol armies invaded Korea in the thirteenth century. The Mongol flute is thought to have a particularly sad tone, a piercing, melancholy sound quality. Chŏng Pyŏng-uk's note on this *sijo* describes the *hoga* as an instrument "made of a dried reed, played by the Mongol people and having an extremely sad sound."[14] So of all the flute melodies that the admiral might have heard on that night, this would have been the saddest. Why? Because it was the flute played by the Mongol invaders, the soldiers of Ogadai Khan, who only rarely visited their homes and whose late-night melancholy was nearly as famous as their prowess in battle. This would have been the flute heard by the Korean defenders of the towns the Mongols laid siege to; the final line thus suggests, in addition to all the preceding, both the deep melancholy of the warrior and Korean anxieties about facing those particular foreign invaders. I suggest that all of these senses are invoked by the phrase *ilsŏng hoga*, as they are by the remarkable reappearance of the same flute in the final chapter of Maxine Hong Kingston's *The Woman Warrior*, "A Song for a Barbarian Reed Pipe":

> The barbarians were primitives. They gathered inedible reeds when they camped along rivers and dried them in the sun. They dried the reeds tied on their flagpoles and horses' manes and tails. Then they cut wedges and holes. They slipped feathers and arrow shafts into the shorter reeds, which became knock-whistles. During battle the arrows whistled, high whirling whistles that suddenly stopped when the arrows hit true. Even when the barbarians missed, they terrified their enemies by filling the air with death sounds, which T'sai Yen had thought was their only music until one night she heard music tremble and rise like desert wind. She walked out of her tent and saw hundreds of barbarians sitting upon the sand, the sand gold under the moon. Their elbows were raised, and they were blowing on flutes. They reached again and again for a high note, yearning toward a high note, which they found at last and held—an icicle in the desert. The music disturbed T'sai Yen; its sharpness and its cold made her ache. It disturbed her so that she could not concentrate on her own thoughts. Night after night the songs filled the desert no matter how many dunes away she walked. She hid in her tent but could not sleep through the sound. Then out of T'sai Yen's tent, which was apart from the others, the barbarians heard a woman's singing, as if to her babies, a song so high and clear, it matched the flutes. T'sai Yen sang about China and her family there. Her words seemed to be Chinese, but the barbarians understood their sadness and anger. . . .[15]

LOOKING WITHIN: THE KISAENG'S SONG

The stories about Admiral Yi and his *sijo* are not intended as history, nor to prove that he was the one who composed the song. As Richard

Rutt indicates, the text's provenance is at best highly conjectural, but whether the story is true or not seems of less importance than the co-existence of story and song. To tell or read them together—to perform them—is to mark the borders of a Korean cultural identity vis-à-vis the Chinese on the land side and the Japanese across the waters. The Chinese phrase adds to the song's resonance, deepening its historical and emotional dimensions in surprising and multifaceted ways. For instance, we may no-tice that the song provides its own instrumental accompaniment.

A widely known *sijo* by the woman entertainer, or *kisaeng*, Hwang Chin-i (sixteenth c.) inscribes an interplay between Chinese and Korean diction. Where the *Tale of Spring Fragrance* played off the hierarchical, male, authoritarian, Confucian, conservative side of Korean society and culture dramatically against the egalitarian, Korean, vernacular, female side, Hwang Chin-i's *sijo* song and its associated story manage to compress into far briefer compass that same bipolar realm.

> Jade Green Stream, don't boast so proud
> of your easy passing through these blue hills.
> Once you have reached the broad sea,
> to return again will be hard.
> While the Bright Moon fills these empty hills,
> why not pause? Then go on, if you will.[16]

青山裡 碧溪水야 수이 감을 자랑마라
一到 滄海하면 다시 오기 어려오니
明月이 滿空山하니 쉬여 간들 엇더리

Even for a reader having no command of the languages, a glance at the original text will show that this *sijo* song is divided into Chinese and Korean halves: the initial hemistiches are Chinese with Korean grammati-cal markers to situate them in the syntax of the lines, while the final hemi-stiches are pure Korean. How does this partitioning of diction resonate with the meaning of Hwang Chin-i's song? The initial Chinese half of each line both names and situates elements of the natural world: Jade Green Stream in the blue hills; arriving at the broad sea; the Bright Moon filling the empty hills. The second half of each line un-names and dis-locates: don't boast; (it is) hard to return; pause and go. The second, Korean half of each line thus subverts the first, Chinese half, or puts in motion what the first half tries to stop. As a single, isolated song, then, this *sijo* might be said to use natural imagery and themes to challenge the Chinese linguistic and cultural hegemony. Korean grammar and syntax subvert the implicit geopolitical imperatives, the territoriality that the Chinese language claims as a system of signs.

There is a story associated with this *sijo* song, as with Yi Sun-sin's. Hwang Chin-i was a *kisaeng* whose sobriquet was Bright Moon. A certain Confucian scholar-official, whose title of office was a homophone for "Jade Green Stream," *Pyŏkkyesu*—or according to other accounts, whose name was Pyŏk Kyesu—boasted that he was immune to the fabled charms of Bright Moon, whose region he was about to travel through. She made up the song, and he fell off his mule in the middle of a stream when he heard it. The story frame makes the natural scenery a pun for the two humans, the man and the woman, the official and the *kisaeng*, the two opposite poles of traditional Korean society. As happens over and over again in Korean folk literature, the cleverness of the vernacular makes the official, stuffy male seem a fool and topples him from his lofty yet precarious perch.

Like a charcoal rubbing of a gravestone or temple bell, Hwang Chin-i's *sijo* song reveals the two halves of Korean culture: not merely the Chinese elements in Korean culture, but the more universally observable division between formal and informal, male and female, ceremonial and satirical, which happens to plot out between the two systems of signs, Chinese and Korean.

YUN SŎN-DO'S FISHERMAN'S CALENDAR

Yun Sŏn-do (1587–1671) is the most studied, and among the most highly revered, of Korean poets. Like Chŏng Ch'ŏl (1536–1593), he encountered numerous political setbacks, including periods of exile. He eventually moved back to his home town, Kyŏngwŏn, where he lived the last years of his life in rustic retirement. Yun's *sijo* sequence "Song of the Five Friends," "*O'u ka*," is admired for the elegant clarity of its statement of a well-established theme in Korean and Chinese poetry, appreciation for the "five friends" of the title: water, rock, pine, bamboo, and the moon. This may seem a less than compelling subject in and of itself, yet its stability as symbol and symbolization of stability endow it with poignant significance when read against the notoriously tumultuous background of history. It was the "former times," after all, in both China and Korea, that had been stable and therefore tranquil. The wistful tone of the final stanza in Yun's sequence would not be unappreciated by the Korean reader, who would know of the political difficulties that Yun had experienced and would also be familiar with other *sijo* compositions, such as those by Chŏng Ch'ŏl, on the same subject.

> Small, rising high
>> to light up all the myriad things.
> In the deep night, you alone
>> are bright. Is there another?
> And though you see, you say nothing.
>> Are you my friend, I fondly hope?[17]

Yun's *Fisherman's Calendar*, *Ŏbu sasi sa*, a forty-verse sequence on another well-established subject in Korean and Chinese literature, describes the tranquil existence of the fisherman in what is widely read as another statement of the theme of rustic retirement from the troubles of official, public life. Yet just as the question at the end of "Song of the Five Friends" raises the issue, if not the specter, of the official realm and thereby injects the disturbances of the public sphere into the tranquil, private zone, the *Fisherman's Calendar* repeatedly interrupts its peaceful excursions by references to the public world of government and political maneuvering. There is the elegant tranquility of stanza 7 from the Spring section, for example:

> Tread on the flowering grasses,
>> pluck the orchids and iris.
> *Beach the boat, beach the boat.*
> What was loaded into
>> the boat small as one leaf?
> *Chigukch'ong, chigukch'ong, ŏsawa.*
> On the way out, nothing but mist;
>> coming back, the moon.[18]

An entire day is compressed between the contrasting images of morning mist and evening moon, a day in which, it would seem, little care or attention is given to the business of fishing, since no fish are carried back. Instead, the speaker takes note of the natural surroundings, the flowers, *fish* only for the truly idle fisherman. The only labor is the launching and rowing of the boat, since the cargo is nothing but mist and moonlight.

Yet the stanzas immediately preceding and following this one add direct references to the troubled public realm:

> Evening light comes slanting;
> > we should stop, and turn back.
> *Lower the sail, lower the sail.*
> The willows and flowers on the banks,
> > each branch, each stem seems new.
> *Chigukch'ong, chigukch'ong, ŏsawa.*
> The high officials would be envious,
> > but why think of the myriad things?[19]

(Spring 6)

> I drank and lay back;
> > the boat carried me down through the shallows.
> *Secure the boat, secure the boat.*
> Pink petals floated near;
> > Towŏn itself must have been near.
> *Chigukch'ong, chigukch'ong, ŏsawa.*
> Red dust of the world,
> > how far away it seemed.[20]

(Spring 8)

The *Calendar* builds its story out of the interplay between the two realms, constructing a double sense of longing, of nostalgia: for the fisherman's excursion and life that constantly ends with the return to shore, and also, perhaps surprisingly given Yun's personal experience, for the conflict-ridden public life he has left behind and yet repeatedly turns back toward.

The *Calendar* is also noteworthy for its formal features. We know, for instance, that the *sijo* is a short verse form, just three lines, with a noticeable balance, rhythmic and rhetorical, between the halves of lines 1 and 2. The third line always begins with a turn of thought or image, and then the composition resolves itself in the remainder of that extended line. But Yun's masterpiece in the *sijo* form traduces almost all of its norms. Where the *sijo* is short, the *Calendar* proceeds through forty verses, deliberately, evenly apportioned among the four seasons. Where the *sijo* has three lines, the *Calendar*'s stanzas each have five, with a work song-like chorus following the second line, urging the boat handlers or the angler to the navigational task, and a purely onomatopoeic line placed before the final line. The beginning of the third line avoids the usual turn and simply continues the narrative, ending the verse without passing through the normally expanded remainder of the line.

Because it results from the relaxation of certain norms and the addition of two lines that are so formulaic they hardly stir the gentle currents of the whole sequence, the impact of Yun's gentle assault on the *sijo* form is difficult to register. A description of the syllabic count of the seventh Spring stanza, translated above, may illustrate. There are four groups in each line of the standard *sijo*, with a syllable count for the first two lines usually in the pattern of 3, 4, 4, 4. The first group in line 3 always has three syllables. The second group almost always has five or more syllables; there are four syllables in group 3, and three syllables in group 4. This syllabic contour in the third line is a distinctive feature of the *sijo* form. In *The Fisherman's Calendar*, however, the patterned variation in syllable counts is relaxed. For "Tread on the flowering grasses," the syllable counts in the four word groups of the first line are 3, 4, 3, 4. For the second line, they are 2, 3, 4, 4. For the third line, Yun's *sijo* completely abolishes the contour (3, 5, 4, 3) and divides the line into two identical pairs: 3, 4; 3, 4, the same pattern as the first line.[21]

In place of the rhetorically and syllabically "plain" stanzas that precede it, the final stanza caps the complete cycle by a flourish of "regular" *ŏssijo:*

Now the day is ending;
time to rest after the banquet.
Make the boat fast. Make the boat fast.

> In ecstasy walk the path
>> where red flowers lie scattered on the wind-blown snow.
>
> *Chigukch'ong, chigukch'ong, ŏsawa.*
> As a frosty moon crosses the western ridge
> lean against the pine sill.

The final stanza of the *Calendar* is a magnificent tour de force.

> The second line of this final stanza . . . much like the second group in
> the last line of the standard (*sijo*) . . . expands; the third line, with its
> much closer adherence to the standard, final-line syllabic pattern, and
> with the rhetorical "turn" on "frosty moon," . . . reestablishes the stan-
> dard *sijo* norm. The final line of this final stanza has the double effect,
> therefore, of returning both that stanza and with it the entire cycle to
> the standard *sijo* norm. . . .[22]

The *Calendar* negotiates its way between the world of seventeenth-
century Korean officialdom and the idealized realm of the rustic fisherman,
like many Chinese and Korean predecessors. It negotiates its way between
folk song and *sijo*, bringing the refrain from the former into the otherwise
undecorated realm of the latter. The second refrain in each stanza—*Chigukch'ong, chigukch'ong, ŏsawa*—uses Chinese-character phrases, some of
which appear in another *sijo* related to fishing and boating, to render the
sounds of rowing.[23] This seems reminiscent of the *hyangch'al* system in
such texts as the *Samguk yusa*, which used Chinese characters to record
the Korean language. The small boat moves away from the banks of the
sijo verse form, but always returns.

TO BE UNDIVIDED

These several *sijo* texts convey a reader or listener on various excursions, by which I mean to evoke both a pleasant, brief journey out and
back and the sense of the term in the physical sciences, "a movement from
and back to a mean position or axis in an oscillating or alternating motion."[24] The *sijo* ascribed to Chŏng Mongju negotiates a movement from

literature and performance to and from history. Its framing narrative records a point of resistance to the shift from one dynasty to another; simultaneously, even as the subject of the song, the loyalist Koryŏ statesman Chŏng Mong-ju, is caused by the Yi faction physically to disappear, the song is left to stand as a bridge from one dynasty to the next. Through the Chinese-language phrase *ilp'yŏn tansim*, the song invokes a standard of absolute constancy even as it subjects the physical embodiment of the ideal to a process of evaporation in the song's Korean-language retort of dying, decay, disintegration, vanishing.

Admiral Yi's *sijo* bridges similar realms: oral and literary, informal narrative and formal history, Chinese and Korean language and culture. The admiral's *sijo* contains the additional nicety of the third line's final gesture, in which the single flute note, originating outside the figure of the admiral perched high on the wall, pierces him to the bowels. The *sijo* literally pins together the exterior and interior realms, the objective and subjective, the determined and the doubtful, the Korean and the other, in much the same way that Ch'ŏyong's song manages to pin together the two nesting narratives of the king of Silla and the son of the dragon king.

Hwang Chin-i's *sijo* song ties together in mutual contrast the formal and informal, the Chinese—literally—and the Korean, the male and the female. If we can entertain the idea that in the story of Ch'ŏyong a woman was made to disappear, the story and *sijo* song by and about Hwang Chin-i will remind us of other stories in the *Samguk yusa* and elsewhere in which women characters possess the full range of capacities for negotiation, resistance, and even for overthrowing the powers that be.

Yun Sŏn-do's *sijo* sequence takes the reader or listener away from the shores of this life into the idealized realm of the rustic fisherman. Repeatedly, regularly, however, in its oscillation through the seasons, the hours of the day, and the alternation from one stanza to the next, the leaf-flat boat of the song brings the story back again. The sequence drifts far from the undemanding formal requirements of the *sijo*, but then in the flourish of the nonstandard, *ŏssijo* final stanza, returns the sequence to the norm at the end.

What are we to make of all this coming and going along the paths through and between so many contrasting realms and into the interior spaces of Korean literary culture? To begin, we should note that the idea of an author is of questionable importance, or rather, that it is important to question the idea of an author for a *sijo* text. Little is known of the woman Hwang Chin-i, and even though much more is known about Yi Sun-sin and Chŏng Mong-ju, little documentation exists that would link either person as author to a given text. In fact, the existing documentation merely points out the many lacunae, most notably chronological, in the record. This suggests, as discussed above, that the *sijo* might be viewed as an oral rather than written form of literature.

The chronological gap between Chŏng Mong-ju's life and the historical period when "his" *sijo* was recorded, from the fourteenth century to the eighteenth, or between his life and the first appearance of the famous phrase *ilp'yŏn tansim* in the Chosŏn dynasty Veritable Records, throws into disorder another common element in literary history, the dates, and with it the possibility or inclination to ask of a text, What does this tell the reader about the historical period when it was written? Because it cannot be established that Chŏng composed the *sijo* in question, the text cannot tell us anything about late Koryŏ history; rather, it seems to reflect a later reading of Korean history—and perhaps more specifically, the illustration of an abstract virtue, loyalty, expressed by the Chinese-language phrase *ilp'yŏn tansim* and its inscription within such stories as the death of Chŏng Mong-ju, the fictional *p'ansori* narrative about Ch'unhyang, or other examples such as the *sijo* texts that use the same phrase on similar and sometimes quite different themes.

If the mixture of such phrases as *ilp'yŏn tansim* with such ideas as loyalty and such exemplary figures as Chŏng Mong-ju or Ch'unhyang were thought of as a kind of cultural stew, a Korean *jjigae*, or more elegantly, perhaps, as a system of circulating cultural signs, then the *sijo* form might be pictured as the ladle that dips out a helping. In this system, the same elements may combine in such disparate forms as the *sijo*, the *p'ansori*, and even the official dynastic records. "Authorship" is not a matter of creation but of association; that is to say, the result not of individual self-expression but of a cultural projection.

Perhaps because the *sijo* texts that we have been considering in this chapter are viewed as so representative of the genre, they also seem to share a common theme, each taking form as a linguistic, literary, cultural entity around an absence or disjuncture. A common enough theme in lyric poetry is separation: being apart from one's love provides the literary occasion to make a sad song. In the stories about the exemplary texts we have been considering, Chŏng Mong-ju was "apart" from the Yi faction that was founding a new dynasty, and in a sense also apart from the dynasty to which he had pledged his loyalty, as its life came to an end at about the same time that his did. As a general, Yi Sun-sin was apart from his men, apart from his country's enemies, and still apart from the day to come, when all would be joined in the battle. As a *kisaeng* woman, Hwang Chin-i was apart from Confucian male society, apart from the boastful official. As an exiled official, Yun Sŏn-do was apart from public life and apart from the real life of the working fisherman. The cultural projection, as I called it, is the unified whole; that is, if these *sijo* begin by engaging a sense of disconnectedness, disjunction, incompleteness, they close up the difference in the strikingly echoed phrases denoting singularity: *one* piece red heart, the loyalty joining Chŏng Mong-ju to the Koryŏ dynasty; *one* note of the Mongol flute, the sound joining Admiral Yi Sun-sin to the vast, invisible expanse of past, present, and future; and *once* reach the wide sea, the distant point in time and space where the stream vanishes into the sea. As a sequence, Yun's *calendar* moves back and forth between the realms of here and there, real and ideal, carried on the boat flat as *one* single leaf— *ilyŏp p'yŏnju*. The desire fulfilled by these *sijo* is to be undivided.

Reflections on the *sijo* in the preceding chapter lead me to concluding observations about the persistent theme of oneness in several well-known examples of the genre. The performance of the *sijo*, the singing of a text but also the telling of the associated story, makes possible the unification of separated entities of some kind. If, as an essentially lyric song, the *sijo* might be said to take shape around an assumed absence or separation, that void is not the mundane absence of a loved one: the absence lies at the heart's core, but not some lonely individual's heart. Given the problems of ascription to individual authors and the broad circulation of the *sijo* texts as symbols of Korean culture rather than merely individual expressions of feeling, the *sijo* songs considered in the previous chapter invite consideration as reflections of Korean culture itself. If in those reflections we notice a yearning for completeness, wholeness, unification, we might think of the song, in its various dimensions of textual identity, performance, mediation between Chinese and Korean linguistic norms, as a bridge between desire and its object.

But this is also the story the plague spirit told to Ch'ŏyong, in which it explained the self-transformation it undertook in order to negotiate the distance, physical as well as semantic, between beauty and desire. Sŏdong's song in the story of King Mu negotiates the same space between desire and possession. That act goes echoing through the later stages of the story as well, as Sŏdong sends the gold, dug out of the ground to make room for the potatoes he planted, back to the parents of his new bride in exchange for the daughter they have lost. What came out of holes in the groom's ground is sent to fill the vacant space in the bride's family. Thus also in the story of Lady Suro, whose desire for the flowers on the high cliff prompts the mysterious old man to climb up, gather them, and present them to her with his "Flower Offering Song": one act between Suro and the old man, negotiating desire and possession, prompts another in which the sea dragon takes away Lady Suro, who possesses both beauty and beautiful flowers. The song that the villagers learn to perform renegotiates the return of the beauty, Lady Suro, but the conclusion of the story resists closure, saying that the interaction of beauty and desire to possess it continued wherever Lady Suro went. The resentment of the party dispossessed in these negotiations figures obliquely: the powerful spirit notices Ch'ŏyong's restraint because it appears in place of anticipated angry resentment; the gold gift balances the loss of the daughter in the story of Sŏdong; Lady Suro's husband asks her, ever so mildly, what happened during her sojourn under the sea.

A similar pattern of desire, possession, negotiation, and renegotiation informs—gives form to—the foundation hymn of the Chosŏn dynasty, the *Song of the Dragons Flying to Heaven*. The desire to take possession, expressed as the denial of it, is the central motif, the organizing theme, of the *Song*. The entire enterprise protests repeatedly that the Yi family ancestors were not motivated by personal ambition to seize possession of the state; rather, heaven intended them to do it and made this plain in various portents, which it would have been wrong of the Yis and their followers to ignore. But to take possession of something is to create a ragged edge in the fabric of ties that bind it to others. The face plate in the story of Ch'ŏyong; the emptying and filling of gaps and spaces in the story of King Mu; the negotiations of gift and the embarrassment caused by incurred obligation in the story of Lady Suro all suggest the precarious nature of the balance struck and the need for additional reassuring signs of its provenance. The massive enterprise of the *Song of the Dragons*—its compilation, translation, promulgation, and repeated performance; its inscription of a Chinese counterpart for each segment of the Korean narrative; the supremely orderly progression of its narrative—suggests that the balance struck was equally precarious, while on a much larger scale. The object of the *Song*, after all, was a disengagement from history, and a shift to the ceremonial ritual for which the *Song* itself constituted the occasion.

The implicit argument of my reading of these texts emerges here: literary texts such as these—records, histories, poems, stories, songs—are social artifacts, not individual creations, and it makes sense to consider them as products of an ongoing process of cultural formation and reformation. As a site of social exchange, such literature is broadly implicated in the ceaseless rounds of negotiations, contracting, and renegotiations through which individuals, groups, clans, and classes struggle to claim or assert identity, authority, and value.

A given text contracts the temporary balance of conflicting claims. Performance reenacts the balance. Repeated performance must suggest a renewed sense of imbalance and provoke the desire to possess once more the beautiful moment of repose, the momentary stay against confusion that Robert Frost asserted is poetry's single, modest purpose.[1]

NOTES

Epigraph: *Hyangga* by the monk Wŏlmyŏng: Pak Sŏng-ŭi, *Han'guk kayo munhangnon kwa sa* (Seoul: Sŏnmyŏn munhwasa, 1974), 115–116.

A BRIEF HISTORY OF KOREAN LITERATURE
TO THE NINETEENTH CENTURY

For general reference, I have used the five-volume (plus index) history of Korean literature by Cho Tong-il, *Han'guk munhak t'ongsa*, 3d ed. (Seoul: Chisik sanŏpsa, 1994).

1. Stephen W. Linton, "Life After Death in North Korea," in David R. McCann, ed., *Korea Briefing: Toward Reunification* (Armonk, N.Y.: M. E. Sharpe, 1997), 90–91.
2. Cho Tong-il 1994, 1:227.
3. Edwin A. Cranston, *A Waka Anthology, Volume One: The Gem-Glistening Cup* (Stanford: Stanford University Press, 1993), 618.
4. See Adrian Buzo and Tony Prince, *Kyunyŏ-jŏn: The Life, Times and Songs of a Tenth-Century Korean Monk* (Honolulu: University of Hawaii Press, 1993).
5. Marshall R. Pihl, "Koryŏ Sŏn Buddhism and Korean Literature," *Korean Studies* 19(1995): *passim.*
6. See Peter H. Lee, *Lives of Eminent Korean Monks* (Cambridge: Harvard University Press, 1969).
7. Cho Tong-il 1994, 2:38f.
8. For the story, see Richard Rutt, *The Bamboo Grove: An Introduction to Sijo* (Ann Arbor: University of Michigan Press, 1998), #56 Note. For the two *sijo*, see page 32 of this book.
9. Ibid., #57 Note.
10. Cho Tong-il 1994, 3:220.
11. See Marshall R. Pihl, *The Korean Singer of Tales* (Cambridge: Harvard-Yenching Institute, 1994), 50.

12. See JaHyun Kim Haboush, *The Memoirs of Lady Hyegyŏng: The Autobiographical Writings of a Crown Princess of Eighteenth-Century Korea* (Berkeley: University of California Press, 1996).

PART ONE: AN ANTHOLOGY OF KOREAN LITERATURE

The *Samguk sagi*

"Song of the Oriole": Chŏng Pyŏng-uk, Han'guk kojŏn sigaron (Seoul: Sin'gu munhwasa, 1994), 52.

The *Samguk yusa*

See note 2 under part 2, "Ch'ŏyong and Manghae Temple: A Parable of Literary Negotiation," below, for a list of editions of the *Samguk yusa*. I have used the Korean-language translation in Yi Chae-ho, *Samguk yusa* (Seoul: Ch'ujinhoe, 1966).

Book 1: Tan'gun (*Ancient Chosŏn*): Yi Chae-ho, *Samguk yusa*, 1:75–77.

Book 2: The Story of Lady Suro: Ibid., 197–199.

Book 2: Ch'ŏyong and Manghae Temple: Ibid., 222–225.

Book 2: King Mu: Ibid., 250–252.

Koryŏ Songs

"Would You Go": Cho Kyu-ik, *Kojŏn munhak kangŭi ch'ongsŏ 1: Koryŏ sogak kasa, kyŏnggi ch'ega, sŏnch'o akchang* (Seoul: Hansaem ch'ulp'an chusik hoesa, 1993), 121–122.

"Song of the Green Mountains": Ibid., 117–118.

HISTORY AS LITERATURE: THE POLITICAL AND CULTURAL TRANSITION FROM KORYŎ TO CHOSŎN

The *Koryŏsa: The History of Koryŏ*

Book 1: "The Ten Injunctions and the Death of Wang Kŏn": Pak Si Hyŏng, Hong Hŭi Yu, trans., Koryŏsa (P'yŏngyang: Kwahakwŏn ch'ulp'ansa, 1962; reprint, Seoul: Yŏgang ch'ulp'ansa, 1991), 1:115–118.

Book 117: "Biographies: Chŏng Mong-ju": Ibid., 315–318.

Song of the Dragons Flying to Heaven

Yi Yun-sŏk, ed., *Wanyŏk Yongbi ŏch'ŏn ka*, 3 vols. (Seoul: Pogosa, 1994).

EARLY CHOSŎN (1392–1598)

Sijo

Reference numbers following the authors' names and dates are entry numbers in Chŏng Pyŏng-uk, ed., *Sijo munhak sajŏn* (Seoul: Sin'gu munhwasa, 1970).

Kasa

"Song to Spring": Yi Sang-bo, ed., *Yijo kasa chŏngsŏn* (Seoul: Ch'ŏjŏng yŏnsa, 1973), 9–12.
"Song of Longing": Ibid., 141–145.
"Song of a Humble Life": Ibid., 195–199.
"Married Sorrow": Kwŏn Tu-hyŏn, ed., *Kojŏn siga: Han'guk munhak ch'ongsŏ 1* (Seoul: Haenaem, 1997), 294–297.

Hanmun: Poems and Prose in Chinese

1. Cho Tong-il 1994, 3:215.
2. Carter J. Eckert et al., *Korea Old and New: A History* (Seoul: Ilchokak Publishers and Korea Institute, Harvard University, 1990), 164.
3. Ch'oe Ik Han and Hong Ki Mun, trans., *Yŏnam chakp'um chip* (P'yŏngyang: Chosŏn chakka tongmaeng ch'ulp'ansa, 1954), 22–23.

Hansi by Yi Kyu-bo and Others:
"To the Master of Kŭmch'ŏn Temple," by Ch'oe Ch'i-wŏn: Hŏ Kyŏng-jin, trans., *Ko Un Ch'oe Ch'i-wŏn sisŏn* (Seoul: P'yŏngminsa, 1996), 60.
"Autumn Night Rain," by Ch'oe Ch'i-wŏn: Ibid., 52.
"At Kwallan Temple," by Kim Pu-sik: Kim Tal-jin, trans., *Han'guk hansi vol. 1* (Seoul: Minŭmsa, 1990), 53.
"White Heron and Smartweed": Hŏ Kyŏng-jin, trans., *Paegun Yi Kyu-bo sisŏn* (Seoul: P'yŏngminsa, 1997), 38.
"To Sambaek, My Son, Drinking Young": Ibid., 47.
"Straw for the Burning": Ibid., 127.
"Two Verses on the Moon in a Well": Ibid., 143.
"Impromptu": Ibid., 163.
"Evening View": Kim Tal-jin, *Han'guk hansi vol. 1,* 96.
"A Wife's Resentment," by Im Che: Ibid., 579.
"Mountain Temple," by Im Che: Ibid.

Hansi by Hŏ Nansŏrhŏn:
"At My Son's Grave": Hŏ Kyŏng-jin, trans., *Hŏ Nansŏrhŏn sisŏn* (Seoul: P'yŏngminsa, 1996), 20.

"Contemplation": Ibid., 16.
"Sending Off": Ibid., 23.
"To My Elder Brother": Ibid., 27.
"The Young Seamstress": Ibid., 37–39.

"The Story of Master Hŏ": Ch'oe Ik Han and Hong Ki Mun, trans., *Yŏnam chakp'um chip* (P'yŏngyang: Chosŏn chakka tongmaeng ch'ulp'ansa, 1954), 11–21.

PART 2: NEGOTIATIONS IN KOREAN LITERATURE

Introduction

1. Elizabeth J. Perry, *Rebels and Revolutionaries in North China, 1845–1945* (Stanford: Stanford University Press, 1980). David R. McCann, "Confrontation in Korean Literature," in Donald N. Clark, ed., *The Kwangju Uprising: Shadows Over the Regime in South Korea* (Boulder: Westview Press, 1988).

Ch'ŏyong and Manghae Temple: A Parable of Literary Negotiation

1. Cho Tong-il, *"Ch'ŏyong kamu ŭi sajŏk ihae,"* in Cho Tong-il, ed., *T'alch'um ŭi yŏksa wa wŏlli* (Seoul: Hongsŏngsa 1988), 13–28.

2. Ha Tae-hung and Grafton K. Mintz, *Samguk yusa* (Seoul: Yonsei University Press, 1972), 126–128. Other translations: Iryŏn, *Samguk yusa*, Ch'oe Nam-sŏn, ed. (Seoul: Minjung Sŏgwan, 1973), 88–89 (a reprint of Ch'oe's 1928 edition). Korean translations include Yi Chae-ho's, in two volumes, in the series *Segye kojŏn chŏnjip* (Seoul: Han'guk kyoyuk ch'ujinhoe, 1966), 222–226, 390–391; Ch'oe Ch'ŏl, *Hyangga ŭi munhakjŏk haesŏk* (Seoul: Yonsei University Press, 1990), 214–216; Pak Sŏng-ŭi, *Han'guk kayo munhangnon kwa sa* (Seoul: Sŏnmyŏng Munhwasa, 1974), 126f.; Kim Pong-du, trans., *Samguk yusa* (Seoul: Kyomunsa, 1993), 180–184. The most exhaustive study of the song itself is Yang Chu-dong, *Koga yŏn'gu*, 6th ed. (Seoul: Ilchogak, 1973), 378–431. In addition to the Ha-Mintz translation into English, an abridged version is found in Peter H. Lee, ed., *Sourcebook of Korean Civilization* (New York: Columbia University Press, 1993), 209–210.

For a useful compendium of articles on the literary aspects of the *Samguk yusa*, see Sin Tong-uk and Kim Yŏl-gyu, eds., *Samguk yusa ŭi munyejŏk yŏn'gu*, 3d ed. (Seoul: Saemunsa, 1993).

3. Chŏng Pyŏng-uk, *"Kodae siga,"* in *Han'guk munhwasa taegye 5* (Seoul: Koryŏ taehak minjok munhwa yŏn'guso, 1971), 764f. See Marcel Granet, *Festivals and Songs of Ancient China* (London: Routledge, 1932).

4. The trajectory of the heroic narrative of early Korean history, especially such texts as SGYS, can be plotted from the late nineteenth-century writings of Sin Ch'ae-

ho and their attack on traditional, Confucianized versions of Korean history and the simultaneous assault by Japanese scholars on the very idea of an independent Korean culture. See Michael Robinson, "National Identity and the Thought of Sin Ch'aeho: *Sadaejuŭi* and *Chuch'e* in History and Politics," *The Journal of Korean Studies* 5 (1984). During the period of the Japanese occupation of Korea, Ch'oe Nam-sŏn added his essays on Korean cultural history, his anthology of *sijo*, his republication of SGYS with a lengthy, cultural nationalist introduction—"a variety of Korean nationalism that upheld the value of Korea's unique cultural and historical traditions as a reaction against the dominance of Japanese government and culture"—(803; citation below), and eventually his writings on *Park* culture, based on his studies of the Tan'gun myth from SGYS. See Chizuko T. Allen, "Northeast Asia Centered Around Korea: Ch'oe Namsŏn's View of History," *The Journal of Asian Studies* 49(4)(November 1990).

5. See Kim Tong-uk, *Han'guk kayo ŭi yŏn'gu* (Seoul: Ulyu Munhwasa, 1961), 121, and Judith Van Zile, "*Ch'oyongmu:* An Ancient Dance Survives," *Korean Culture* 8(2)(1987): 13.

6. For an overview, see Cho Tong-il, *Han'guk munhak t'ongsa*, 2d ed. (Seoul: Chisik Sanŏpsa, 1990), 1:213.

7. Chŏng Pyŏng-uk, article; source unknown. (I have not been able to locate the article in question. I read it in 1973–74 while conducting my dissertation research in Seoul. I was fortunate at that time to have been able to meet with the late Professor Chŏng, and to attend his class on Korean literature at Seoul National University.)

8. Ch'oe Ch'ŏl, *Hyangga ŭi munhakchŏk haesŏk* (Seoul: Yonsei University Press, 1990), 214–216.

9. Cho Tong-il 1990, 213; Boudewijn Walraven, *Muga: The Songs of Korean Shamanism* (Leiden, 1985), 38.

10. Ch'oe, SGYS, 126; Kim Pong-du, SGYS, 276–277; Ha-Mintz, SGYS, 186.

11. Kim Yong-ok, *Samguk yusa intŭk* (Seoul: T'ongnamu, 1992), 1113.

12. The various Classical Chinese dictionaries such as Morohashi, Giles, Karlgren, and others give a range of meanings for the word *mi*, from *umai, utsukushii, yoi, medetai, yomisuru* in Morohashi to *admirable, fine, beautiful* in Giles, to *fine, beautiful, excellent* in Karlgren. In combination with the word for *woman, nyŏ*, however, the range of meanings collapses to *beautiful.* Cf. Herbert A. Giles, *A Chinese-English Dictionary*, Vol. 1 (New York: Paragon, 1964), #7727 and #4546; Bernhard Karlgren, *Analytic Dictionary of Chinese and Sino-Japanese* (New York: Dover, 1974), 88; *Dai kanwa jiten Vol. 9* (Tokyo: Morohashi, 1985), 57f. This full range of meanings is comprised by the word as it is used in the story of the monk Hyesuk (SGYS 4, 2.2). Hyesuk accompanies the *hwarang* knight Kugam on a hunting trip, and at the banquet that follows the successful hunt, surveys the table, then turns and tells the huntsman that he has some meat even more delicious, fresh, tasty, tempting—in a word, more *mi*—for him to try. When Kugam replies that he wants to try it, Hyesuk slices some of his own flesh from his thigh and sets it before him. This act reverses the semantic

field of *mi*, needless to say, as the *hwarang* knight learns true compassion for all living creatures from the gruesome experience. (The Ha-Mintz translation, page 294, translates *mi* as *delicious:* " 'I have some meat more delicious than this,' Hyesuk said. 'May I serve it to you?' ")

13. Choi Sun-u, *5000 Years of Korean Art* (Seoul: Hyonam Publishing, 1979), 349. Also see K. C. Chang, *Art, Myth, and Ritual: The Path to Political Authority in Ancient China* (Cambridge: Harvard University Press, 1983), 65f. on "God's agents of the four directions."

14. Cho Tong-il 1988, 20, notes the omission, without explanation. Ch'ŏyong might have been facing west in his confrontation with the spirit.

15. Such questions are the rhetorical frames through which the speaker is authorized to proceed. A conflation of verbal riddling and mirrors underlies the ceremony from Book 1, Chapter 17 of the Japanese *Kojiki*, when the sun goddess Amaterasu, who has concealed herself in a cave, is lured out by a ceremony of singing, dancing, laughter, and ribaldry performed by the other deities.

> Then Takama-Nō-Para shook as the eight hundred deities laughed all at once.
>
> Then Ama-Terasu-Opo-Mi-Kamii, thinking this strange, opened a crack in the heavenly rock-cave door, and said from within:
>
> "Because I have shut myself in, I thought that Takama-Nō-Uzume would be completely dark. But why is it that Amē-Nō-Uzume sings and dances, and all the eight hundred deities laugh?"
>
> Then Amē-Nō-Uzume said:
>
> "We rejoice because there is here a deity superior to you."
>
> While she was saying this, Amē-Nō-Ko-Yane-Nō-Mikōtō and Puto-Tama-Nō-Mikōtō brought out the mirror and showed it to Ama-Terasu-Opo-Mi-Kamii.
>
> Then Ama-Terasu-Opo-Mi-Kami, thinking this more and more strange, gradually came out of the door and approached [the mirror].

The deities then seal Amaterasu out of the cave by placing a rope behind her. Donald L. Philippi, trans., *Kojiki* (Princeton: Princeton University Press and Tokyo University Press, 1969), 84–85.

For an intriguing notice of the verbal conflation of a mirror and seal, see Marc Shell, *Money, Language, and Thought* (Baltimore: The Johns Hopkins University Press, 1982): "At a magic mirror before which he stands in Part One, Faust sees the image (*Bild*) of a beautiful woman. . . . The heart of Faust, indeed, is soon impressed (*geprägt*) by the image of Gretchen" (111); "when the besieged Emperor appears on stage, he expresses fear that he acted wrongly in making paper money . . . and again describes his experience at the end of the masque. In the casket, he says, he saw a mirrorlike source (*Quelle*) that revealed to him a counter-emperor. Somehow his own breast was sealed. 'I felt my breast sealed (*besiegelt*) when I stood mirrored (*bespiegelt*) in that fiery realm' (119).'' Shell notes this play of *seal* against *mirror* in his analysis of Faust's effort to appropriate Helen as a symbol of classical Greek: "the German Faust . . . wants to appropriate to himself the Greek Helen" (115).

Such textual mirrors also prompt the scholars to perform, as Cho Tong-il noted.

16. Henri Maspero, *China in Antiquity* (Amherst: University of Massachusetts Press, 1978), 116–117. Also see Carmen Blacker, *The Catalpa Bow: A Study of Shamanistic Practices in Japan* (London: Allen and Unwin, 1975), 28: "The *Kojiki* too, compiled in the early eighth century, contains a description of the consort of the Emperor, later to become Empress Jingo, who by means of a ritual became possessed by several deities, transmitting their warnings and instructions through her mouth."

17. On the plague spirit, see Jane Marie Law, "Of Plagues and Puppets: On the Significance of the Name Hyakudayū in Japanese Religion," *The Transactions of the Asiatic Society of Japan*, fourth series, vol. 8, 1993. Law raises the suggestive possibility of a link between Korea and the Hyakudayū deity in the Hachiman cult (127–128) at the time of a smallpox epidemic.

18. See, for example, Alexander Coburn Soper, III, *The Evolution of Buddhist Architecture in Japan* (Princeton: Princeton University Press, 1942), 29: "As a place for worship of the Buddha, [Hōryūji] contains only three buildings of religious purpose: the pagoda which houses His relic, the 'golden' hall in which His image is worshipped, and the lecture hall in which His teachings are expounded. In comparison with later temples, in which the number of such halls was greatly increased in order to provide for the adoration of especially popular deities . . ."

19. See Laurel Kendall, "Wood Imps, Ghosts, and Other Noxious Influences: The Ideology of Affliction in a Korean Village," *The Journal of Korean Studies* 3(1981): 129: "The household gods are encoded into the structure of the house itself. The House Lord (*sŏngju*) resides in the main roof beam, the Birth Grandmother (*samsin, chesŏk*) lives in the inner room, the House-site Official (*t'ŏju taegam*) is enthroned by the back chimney flue. There are minor gods in every room, by the pump, and in the toilet shed. The household is a polity; the gods constitute a government maintaining domestic tranquility and defending the borders against incursions from without."

20. Gail Holst-Warhaft, *Dangerous Voices: Women's Laments and Greek Literature* (London: Routledge, 1992), 118. For reviews of Holst-Warhaft's book, see: Sheila M. Colwell in *Bryn Mawr Classical Review* 4(5)(October 1993); Margaret Alexiou, *Journal of the Hellenic Diaspora* 20(2)(1994); John Rexine, *Ancient World* (1993); Laurie Kain Hart, *The International Greek Folklore Society* 11(3)(May–June 1994).

21. Ibid., 119.

22. Ibid., 156 *et passim*.

23. Ibid., 136f.

24. Aeschylus, *Oresteia*, David Greene and Richmond Lattimore, eds. (Chicago: University of Chicago Press, 1953), 158–159.

25. Ibid., 158.

26. Holst-Warhaft, *Dangerous Voices*, 153–154.

27. *Oresteia*, 163.

28. Ibid.

29. Ibid., 166–167.

30. Compare with J. M. Law, "Of Plagues and Puppets," 123: "The body of the text [*A Reduced Size Copy of the Smallpox Protecting Deity in the Genuine Handwriting of the Venerable Kōtaku*] narrates the following case describing the origins of the worship of Hyakudayū as the plague spirit: *According to the oracle, before a person manifests smallpox, one should put up a protective talisman of (this) deity in various places. . . . The oracle says that in the event of smallpox, one should quickly call the priest of the Hyakudayūden to present the protective talismans.*"

31. Carole Pateman, *The Sexual Contract* (Stanford: Stanford University Press, 1988), 39.

32. Ibid., 41.

33. A comparable pattern is noted in an article about more recent, American institutional history. Laurel Thatcher Ulrich, "Harvard's Womanless History," *Harvard Magazine* 102(2)(1999): 51–59, writes about not just the marginalization of women in histories of the university; she observes further that even when women do appear, the narrative reduces them to mere points by using the word *first*, in the same way that the word *beautiful* is used in the story of Ch'ŏyong. Ulrich cites the example of the centennial-year issues of *Harvard Magazine*: "Six entries include pictures of women, but in only one case—the photograph of Radcliffe president Martina Horner signing a 'non-merger merger' agreement with Harvard president Derek Bok in 1971—are women portrayed as actually doing anything. Harvard men build buildings, conquer disease, play football, appoint cabinets . . . but the women pictured are distinguished only because they were the 'first' of something. In 1904, 'Helen Keller became Radcliffe's first blind graduate.' . . ."

SONG OF THE DRAGONS FLYING TO HEAVEN: NEGOTIATING HISTORY

1. M. M. Bakhtin, *The Dialogic Imagination: Four Essays*, Michael Holquist, ed. (Austin: University of Texas Press, 1996), 272.

2. Han Yŏn-su and Kim Pong-gun, eds., *Hairait'ŭ munhak chasŭbsŏ* (Seoul: Chihaksa, 1993), 212: "It is well known that, because of the didacticism of the genre, the literary quality is not high."

3. Yi Yun-sŏk, ed., *Wanyŏk yongbi ŏch'ŏn ka*, 3 vols. (Seoul: Pogosa, 1994), 1:6–7.

4. Richard Wilhelm, trans., *The I Ching or Book of Changes* (Princeton: Princeton University Press, 1967), 9, 364.

5. Ibid., 9–10.

6. Yi, *Wanyŏk*, 1:7.

7. Ibid., 7–17.

8. See above, "The Ten Injunctions and the Death of the Founder, Wang Kŏn."

9. Yi, *Wanyŏk*, 1:11–13.

10. See previous chapter, "*Ch'ŏyong and Manghae Temple:* A Parable of Literary Negotiation," p. 109.

11. Pak Si Hyŏng, Hong Hŭi Yu, trans., *Koryŏsa*. 11 vols. (P'yŏngyang: Tong P'yŏngyang Inswae Kongjang, 1962; reprint, Seoul: Pogosa, 1994), 1:40.

12. For more detail on a reading of late Koryŏ and early Chosŏn history as a hidden history of violent struggle, see my "Performing *Dragons:* The Construction of a Korean Classical Moment," in Gail Holst-Warhaft and David R. McCann, eds., *The Classical Moment: Views from Seven Literatures* (Lanham, Md.: Rowman and Littlefield, 1999), 105–108.

13. See above, p. 39.

14. Gail Holst Warhaft, *Dangerous Voices: Womens Laments and Classical Greek Literature*, 4–6 and *passim*.

15. See Peter H. Lee, *Songs*, 86 re the term *ttŭt* as it is used in the closing section of admonitions.

16. Yi, *Wanyŏk*, 1:13.

17. See Marshall R. Pihl, *The Korean Singer of Tales* (Cambridge: Harvard-Yenching Institute Monograph Series, 1994), 85–87, 96–99; Kichung Kim, *An Introduction to Classical Korean Literature: From Hyangga to P'ansori* (Armonk, N.Y.: M. E. Sharpe, 1996), 200–203; Cho Tong-il and Kim Hŭng-gyu, eds., *P'ansori ŭi ihae* (Seoul: Ch'angjak kwa pip'yŏngsa, 1979), 19–22. For a splendid modern version of the *p'ansori*-style narrative, see Ch'ae Man-Sik's *Peace Under Heaven*, trans. Chun Kyung-Ja (Armonk, N.Y.: M. E. Sharpe, 1993). The passage beginning "There's an old saying" on page 66 is an example of the narrative aside, and there are many other such passages elsewhere in the novel.

18. Cho Tong-il 1994, 2:287.

19. Ibid., 285.

20. Han and Kim, *Hairaitŭ*, 214.

21. Ki-Moon Lee, "The Inventor of the Korean Alphabet," in Young-Key Kim Renaud, ed., *The Korean Alphabet: Its History and Structure* (Honolulu: University of Hawaii Press, 1997), 25 f.

22. Yi, *Wanyŏk*, 1:147–149.

23. See above, pp. 33–36.

24. Yi, *Wanyŏk*, 3:239.

25. Ibid., 239–240.

26. Wen C. Fong, "Imperial Portraiture of the Ming Dynasty," in Wen C. Fong and James C. Wyatt, eds., *Possessing the Past: Treasures from the National Palace Museum, Taipei* (New York: Abrams, 1996), 332.

PERFORMANCE AND KOREAN *SIJO* VERSE: NEGOTIATING DISTANCE

1. Younghill Kang, *The Grass Roof* (New York: Scribner's, 1951), 28.

2. Ibid., 39.

3. See above, p. 34.

4. Vincent S. R. Brandt, *A Korean Village: Between Farm and Sea* (Cambridge: Harvard University Press, 1971), 25–26.

5. Sin Chae-hyo, ed., *P'ansori sasŏl chip* (Seoul: Minjungsŏgwan, 1972), 7 (for quoted remark) and *passim*. For an English translation, see Richard Rutt and Kim Chong-un, trans., *Virtuous Women: Three Classic Korean Novels* (Seoul: Korean National Commission for UNESCO, 1974).

6. Yi Ka-wŏn, ed., *Ch'unhyang ch'ŏn* (Seoul: Chŏngŭmsa, 1958), 211. The passage in the story uses the same term, *ttŭt*, that is used in the *Song of the Dragons Flying to Heaven* to broach the question of meaning. See above, pp. 129f.

7. Entries in Chŏng Pyŏng-uk, *Sijo munhak sajŏn* (Seoul: Sin'gu munhwasa, 1970).

8. *Kungyŏk chosŏn wangjo sillok* (Seoul: Seoul System, 1997).

9. The edition of Chŏng Mong-ju's *munjip* published in the series *Han'guk myŏng-jŏ taejŏnjip*, Yi Han-jo, trans. (Seoul: Taeyang sŏjŏk, 1975), 25 places the *sijo* song by Chŏng Mong-ju, as well as the *sijo* by Yi Pang-wŏn, at the beginning of the collection. The two *sijo* and the accompanying brief story of the encounter between Chŏng and Yi are said to be recorded in an otherwise unidentified *Miscellany*, or *yusa*. This edition then proceeds to the first entry in the reprinted version of Chŏng's *munjip*, a poem about a journey and visit having nothing to do with the *tansim ka*. See Yi Ch'un-hŭi, ed., *Koryŏ myŏnghyŏn chip* (Seoul: Sŏngkyun'gwan taehakkyo taedongmunhwa yŏn'guso, 1973), 231. One might assume from the first edition, incorrectly, that the *sijo* were part of the *munjip*, Chŏng Mong-ju's collected writings.

10. See above, p. 39.

11. Rutt 1971, 17–18.

12. Chŏng 1970, #2267.

13. Rutt 1971, 18.

14. Chŏng 1971, #528 Note.

15. Maxine Hong Kingston, *The Woman Warrior: Memoirs of a Childhood Among Ghosts* (New York: Vintage, 1977), 242–243. Reprinted by permission of the publisher.

16. Chŏng 1971, #2056.

17. Ibid., #1816. For the other *sijo* in the sequence, see above, pp. 51–52.

18. Ibid., #866.

19. Ibid., #1136.

20. Ibid., #2169.

21. For a more detailed treatment of Yun's *sijo*, see David R. McCann, *Form and Freedom In Korean Poetry* (Leiden: E. J. Brill, 1988), 20–22.

22. McCann 1988, 22.

23. Note in Chŏng 1971, 849.

24. *The American Heritage Dictionary* (Boston: Houghton Mifflin, 1985), 474.

CONCLUSION

1. Robert Frost, "The Figure a Poem Makes: An Introduction," in *Robert Frost, Poetry and Prose*, Edward Connery Latham and Lawrence Thompson, eds. (New York: Holt, 1984), 394.

BIBLIOGRAPHY

The following is a list of books in English that will serve as a good first round of continued reading in pre-modern Korean literature.

Ha Tae-hung and Grafton Mintz. *Samguk Yusa*. Seoul: Yonsei University Press, 1972.

Haboush, JaHyun Kim. *The Memoirs of Lady Hyegyŏng: The Autobiographical Writings of a Crown Princess of Eighteenth-Century Korea*. Berkeley and Los Angeles: University of California Press, 1996.

Kim Hunggyu. *Understanding Korean Literature*. Armonk, N.Y. and London: M. E. Sharpe, 1997.

Kim Jong-gil. *Slow Chrysanthemums: Classical Korean Poems in Chinese*. London: Anvil Press, 1987.

Kim, Kichung. *An Introduction to Classical Korean Literature: From Hyangga to P'ansori*. Armonk, N.Y. and London: M. E. Sharpe, 1996.

Kim-Renaud, Young-Key, ed. *The Korean Alphabet: Its History and Structure*. Honolulu: University of Hawai'i Press, 1997.

Lee, Peter H., ed. *Anthology of Korean Literature From Early Times to the Nineteenth Century*. Honolulu: University of Hawai'i Press, 1981.

———. *Songs of Flying Dragons: A Critical Reading*. Cambridge: Harvard University Press, 1975.

———. *Pine River and Lone Peak: An Anthology of Three Chosŏn Dynasty Poets*. Honolulu: University of Hawai'i Press, 1991.

Lee, Sung-Il. *The Moonlit Pond: Korean Classical Poems in Chinese*. Port Townsend, Wa.: Copper Canyon Press, 1998.

McCann, David R. *Form and Freedom in Korean Poetry*. Leiden: E. J. Brill, 1988.

O'Rourke, Kevin. *Singing Like a Cricket, Hooting Like an Owl: Selected Poems of Yi Kyu-bo*. Ithaca: Cornell East Asia Series, 1995.

———. *Tilting the Jar, Spilling the Moon: Poems from Koryo, Choson, and Contemporary Korea*. Seoul: Universal Publications Agency, 1989.

Pai, Inez Kong. *The Ever White Mountain: Korean Lyrics in the Classical Sijo Form.* Tokyo: Weatherhill, 1965.

Pihl, Marshall R. *The Korean Singer of Tales.* Cambridge: Harvard-Yenching Institute Monograph Series, 1994.

Rutt, Richard and Kim Chong-un. *Virtuous Women: Three Classical Korean Novels.* Seoul: National Commission for UNESCO, 1974.

Rutt, Richard. *The Bamboo Grove: An Introduction to Sijo.* Ann Arbor: University of Michigan Press, 1998.

INDEX OF NAMES AND TITLES

SUBJECT INDEX